THE BLUE BOOK OF STATIONERY

THE

Blue Book

OF

STATIONERY

THE DEFINITIVE GUIDE TO SOCIAL AND BUSINESS CORRESPONDENCE ETIQUETTE

Updated and revised with the guidance of
Pamela Eyring and Robert Hickey
The Protocol School of Washington®

CRANE & CO.

The Blue Book of Stationery:
The Definitive Guide to Social and Business Correspondence Etiquette
Third Edition

Produced by: Jen Rork Design, Inc.
Editor: Amanda R. Haar
Proofreader: Marisa Crumb

Third Edition updated and revised with the guidance and input of:
Pamela Eyring, Owner and Director
Robert Hickey, Deputy Director
The Protocol School of Washington®
Washington, DC: 202-575-5600
Toll free: 877-766-3757
www.psow.com

Titles and forms of address in this edition are updated and revised courtesy
of *Honor & Respect: The Official Guide to Names, Titles, and Forms of Address*
by Robert Hickey, ISBN 978-0-615-19806-4

Published by Crane & Co., Inc.
30 South Street
Dalton, MA 01226
www.crane.com

ISBN 978-0-615-27921-3

Foreword

Common sense and consideration
should be the basis of etiquette and good manners.
—John Quincy Adams

John Quincy Adams had it right. Common sense and consideration should be basis of etiquette and good manners.

However, in today's world, where new means of communication are constantly emerging, it seems that people often sacrifice common sense and consideration for the sake of keeping current.

As the director of The Protocol School of Washington, it's my business to impart an understanding of the finer points of image and etiquette to our students so that they'll find success in both their business and personal lives. Year after year, one of the most important things I teach my students is this: No matter how newfangled or highspeed the latest means of communication might be, nothing outshines the timelessness and sincerity of a well-thought-out piece of correspondence on fine stationery.

Be it a simple thank you for a gift or an important follow-up to a business meeting or interview, a well-composed and presented letter leaves an impression that's far more lasting and impactful than an email or, worse, a voice mail. A letter speaks not just to the matter at hand but to you as a person. It demonstrates a level of sincerity and commitment to the individual you're corresponding with, and, perhaps more important, an understanding of proper etiquette.

At its core, etiquette revolves around three basic building blocks. The first, as Mr. Adams noted, is common sense. The second and third are courtesy and usage.

Common sense dictates what information is included in any correspondence. On an invitation, for example, there is essential information that must be conveyed if you want your guests to show up at your event. Your guests need to know who is inviting them to what function. They also need to know the date, time, and place. A properly worded invitation contains all of that information and presents it succinctly and coherently.

Courtesy is the spirit of etiquette. Its inherent generosity makes for better and more rewarding relationships and it imposes upon us an obligation to be considerate of others. While using this book, you may come across some guidelines that, if followed, you feel might offend someone you love. When that is the case, courtesy demands that you find an alternative. Etiquette is proper only when it facilitates and strengthens relationships.

The third building block is usage. Etiquette has evolved over the years and will continue to evolve. Many of the customs that were proper fifty years ago are anachronisms today. Take wedding invitations for example.

Not very long ago, reply cards were considered improper, even offensive and insulting. Formal invitations were always answered in one's own handwriting on one's own stationery. As our lives became busier and busier, many of us no longer had the time to sit down and handwrite a reply.

Since hosts and hostesses could not risk not receiving responses, they began to send reply cards with their invitations. The courtesy extended to their guests was a common-sense approach to the problem of late and never-received responses. As more and more invitations were sent with reply cards, reply cards became more and more acceptable. Today, they are sent with almost every wedding invitation.

In other words, at some point the traditional way of responding to wedding invitations was not working. Common sense suggested that a solution be developed. The solution was simple: Extend to guests the courtesy of providing them with an easy-to-use card with a stamped, pre-addressed envelope. This solution worked and through its usage reply cards are now perfectly proper and even expected.

Without a doubt, demonstrating an understanding of the etiquette of social and business correspondence can enhance the quality of the relationships you build in your life. For the past twenty years I've relied on *The Blue Book of Stationery* to guide my students through both the solid and subtle rules of correspondence etiquette. It has become a trusted resource to many. But like the rules of etiquette, it is subject to change.

I'm thrilled that Crane & Co. has chosen to publish a third edition of this valuable volume at this time. With this edition's new and expanded content, I feel even better prepared to help my students find ways to successfully blend timeless social graces with today's customs and technology.

You'll want to keep it close at hand whenever you're crafting a piece of correspondence. Within its pages you'll find solid advice on everything from choosing the right type of stationery to use for a given occasion, to how to properly address everyone from a diplomat to a distant cousin.

As you do so, remember that every letter you write, every business card you hand out, and every invitation you issue, is a representation of you. Let etiquette guide you in your choices but always let the true you show through.

Pamela Eyring

Owner and Director
The Protocol School of Washington
www.psow.com

Contents

CHAPTER FIVE: INVITATIONS TO SOCIAL OCCASIONS   119

CHAPTER SIX: RECEPTION AND ENTERTAINMENT STATIONERY   147

CHAPTER SEVEN:
SOCIAL ANNOUNCEMENTS, CORRESPONDENCE, AND CARDS   155

CHAPTER EIGHT: FORMS OF ADDRESS   169

CHAPTER NINE: ABOUT CRANE & CO., INC.   179

INDEX   181

CHAPTER ONE

Social Stationery

Your social stationery wardrobe speaks volumes about you. It's your voice, your presence, when you can't be there to express your gratitude to a loved one or to share a special moment with a friend. When you create and assemble a stationery wardrobe, it's important to keep in mind the impression you hope to make. Your stationery should reflect both your personality and the type of correspondence that you are sending.

Creating a stationery wardrobe requires asking yourself three important questions:

1. What kind of paper should I use?
2. What should I have printed on my stationery?
3. What type of printing should I use for my stationery?

The remainder of this chapter will attempt to answer those questions and help you select the stationery wardrobe that is most appropriate for you.

WHAT KIND OF PAPER SHOULD I USE?

This is actually a three-part question, as you need to choose the material from which the paper is made, the color, and the types of stationery.

Paper is made from either cotton or wood. The first true papers were made from cotton almost two thousand years ago. Wood-pulp papers came into being in the 1800s during the Industrial Revolution. They supplanted cotton-fiber papers for many uses because of their lower cost and the seemingly endless supply of trees.

The finest paper, though, is made from cotton. Before you order your stationery, run your fingers across the paper. Stationery made from cotton will have a soft, rich feel. You will undoubtedly recognize its inherent quality. One hundred percent cotton fibers create the touch and feel of Crane's uncommonly beautiful papers.

Cotton papers are the ideal choice for stationery that is to be engraved or letterpressed. Because cotton fibers are soft and strong, they fully absorb and accept the deep impressions created through these printing processes. The inherent elegance and artistic qualities of both printing methods are truly best displayed and appreciated on 100% cotton paper.

Stationery comes in many different colors. White and ecru—also known as buff, cream, and ivory—are the most popular but grey, blue, pink, yellow, and other colors are also available and increasing in popularity. You can order

· POINTS OF STYLE ·

Earth-Friendly and Everlasting

Concern for the environment is becoming increasingly important among today's consumers. One's choice of paper for stationery, invitations, and business correspondence is no exception.

Crane's 100% cotton papers are ideal for those looking for an environmentally responsible paper that doesn't sacrifice quality. Not a single tree falls to make Crane's 100% cotton paper. Crane uses cotton fibers recovered from the cotton-ginning and cottonseed-oil industries; fibers that otherwise would be discarded. Crane papers are both elegant and earth-friendly.

Cotton fibers are inherently white and are almost pure cellulose. They require fewer chemicals and produce less waste than other raw materials for papermaking. As a result, letters, invitations, and announcements on Crane paper will retain their beauty for generations to come.

several different types of stationery. The two most basic are one for writing notes and one for writing longer letters. While these are essential, you may wish to add variations of these two as you build your stationery wardrobe. We will discuss different types of stationery in detail later in this chapter.

WHAT SHOULD I HAVE PRINTED
ON MY STATIONERY?

How you personalize your stationery depends on the purpose for which the stationery will be used and on what is aesthetically pleasing to you.

Traditionally, stationery features either your name, your name and address, just your address, your monogram, or even your family crest. However, today it's not uncommon for stationery to feature an email address, a website URL, or even a Facebook page.

Again, this is your personal stationery. You should include what you feel best represents you as an individual.

For more on monograms, see page 10.

Sample of a calling card with
an email address

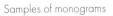

Samples of monograms

WHAT TYPE OF PRINTING SHOULD I USE FOR MY STATIONERY?

Today there are more printing options for personal stationery than ever before. Each method offers its own advantages, ranging from quality to convenience, and lends its own sense of style to each piece of stationery you create.

Engraving is one of the oldest and most beautiful processes for reproducing images on paper. The appeal of engraving lies in the exquisite detail created by its three-dimensional impression. Engraving is produced when the copy is etched in reverse into a copper plate. Ink is deposited in the resulting cavity. The engraving press then forces the paper into the cavity, creating a raised impression. The paper is literally raised with the ink adhering to the raised surface. The fact that the paper is raised is what distinguishes engraving from thermography and lithography.

Engraved stationery is more expensive than thermographed or lithographed stationery. However, much of the price difference lies in the initial cost of the engraving plate. Since engraving plates can be used over and over again, subsequent orders of engraved stationery will cost only a little more than other types of stationery.

It is easy to tell whether a piece of stationery is engraved. Simply turn it over. If there is an indentation (caused by the pressure from the engraving press), it is engraved. You can also tell by looking closely at the impression on the front. The paper will be smoother and there may be a little ripple to the sheet. This is called the "bruise" and is a natural part of the process.

Blind-embossing (or just "embossing") is a process similar to engraving. A raised impression is created from a copper plate. But unlike engraving, no ink is used. Blind-embossing is commonly used for a family coat of arms, the return address on the flap of a wedding envelope, and monogrammed thank-you notes.

Letterpress began in Europe in the 14th century as an alternative to laborious calligraphy. It involves setting type in reverse on a letterpress plate, inking the plate, and then pressing it to the surface of the paper. The raised printing surfaces on the letterpress plate leave a deep impression on the paper. The depth of the image is accentuated by the ink and the minute shadows created within the impression. Letterpress offers a warmth and quality that is not easily duplicated by other printing methods.

Thermography is sometimes called "raised printing." Unlike engraving—where the paper is actually raised—the raise in thermography is created by a resinous powder melted over the flat-printed ink. Thermography is less expensive than engraving and can give your stationery a look similar to—but not quite as nice as—engraving.

Lithography, also known as flat or offset printing, uses ink to print lettering or images onto paper. Lithography is the printing process most commonly used for mass-produced items such as posters, books, and newspapers. The finished product has a flat finish as opposed to the raised or indented finishes of engraved or letterpressed items.

A top-of-the-line home printer is also a viable option for creating personalized stationery. At-home printing is a cost-effective way to make multiple versions of stationery—perhaps personal and business versions—in small quantities. It's particularly ideal for individuals who will need to update their contact information due to a change of address, email, or name. While at-home printing cannot match the look and feel of engraving or letterpress, it is an appropriate choice for some types of correspondence.

SOCIAL STATIONERY FOR WOMEN

There are numerous options when choosing what paper to use for correspondence. While the nature of your correspondence typically dictates the format, there's still plenty of flexibility in color, motif, and other design options.

For Letter Writing

LETTER SHEETS: Letter sheets are the most formal papers in a woman's stationery wardrobe. Measuring $6^{3}/_{8}$" × $8^{1}/_{2}$", letter sheets have a fold along the left-hand side and fold again from top to bottom to fit inside an envelope that is approximately half their size.

Blank, unadorned letter sheets are used to reply to formal invitations and for letters of condolence. Because of their simple elegance, letter sheets may be used for any type of correspondence. Letter sheets may be adorned with a coat of arms, a monogram, a name, an address, or simply left blank.

When using letter sheets, you start on the front page of the letter sheet, followed by page 3. Neither page 2 nor page 4 are written on. Some women prefer to start letter-sheet letters on page 1. Then they open up the letter sheet, turn it sideways and write lengthwise across pages 2 and 3.

CORRESPONDENCE SHEETS: Correspondence sheets, also called "half sheets," are single sheets of stationery, $6^3/_8$" × $8^1/_2$", that fold in half to fit their envelopes. They may be embellished with your monogram, name, address, or name and address. Only the front of a correspondence sheet is written on. If you need additional space, use blank second sheets.

MONARCH SHEETS: Monarch sheets, also known as "executive stationery," are used for general social correspondence and personal business letters. Monarch sheets measure $7^1/_4$" × $10^1/_2$" and fold into thirds to fit their envelopes.

A name, address, or name and address appear at the top of the sheet. Writing should only appear on the front of the sheet. If you need additional space, use blank second sheets.

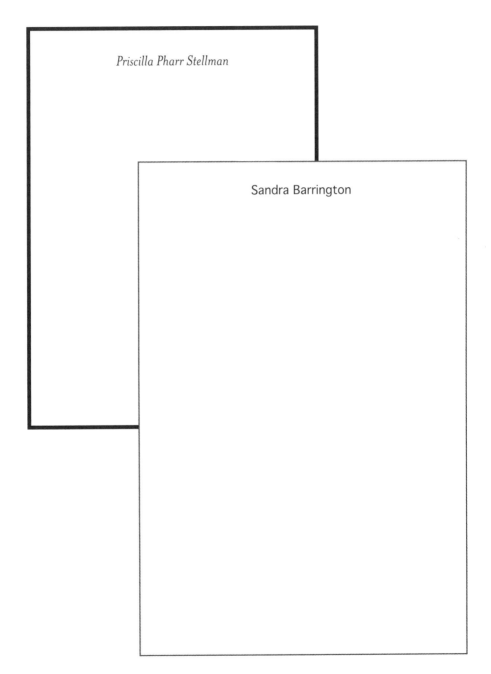

· POINTS OF STYLE ·

Boxed Sets

Circumstances don't always allow for the creation of personalized stationery. In these instances, a quality boxed set is a completely acceptable choice.

Boxed sets are available with preprinted initials, "thank you," or a wide assortment of motifs.

Boxed sets are ideal when time is of the essence or an anticipated change of circumstance (i.e. name change, new address, etc.) is pending. In addition, boxed sets make ideal hostess and going away gifts.

For Note Writing

FOLDED NOTES: Folded notes are used to write thank-you notes, extend informal invitations, and send short messages to friends and acquaintances. The most traditional folded notes would have a woman's full social name centered on the front. However, it is now common for folded notes to have a monogram or a couple's name presented as "Mr. and Mrs." For single women or those who choose to keep their maiden name, "Ms." may be used in place of "Mrs." or "Miss." "Ms." may be used with either the last name alone or with the full name.

For more casual correspondence, it is appropriate to use your first and last name.

The message on a folded note begins on page 1 when the imprint is at the top of the note. The note continues on page 3. When the imprint is in the center of the note, the entire message is written on page 3. Pages 2 and 4 are not normally used, but it's perfectly acceptable to use page 4 if you find yourself writing longer than you had anticipated. After all, you're using fine stationery and it shouldn't be wasted.

CORRESPONDENCE CARDS: One of the most useful items in a stationery wardrobe is the correspondence card. Less formal than a note, these increasingly popular items are used for thank-yous, informal invitations, and short notes.

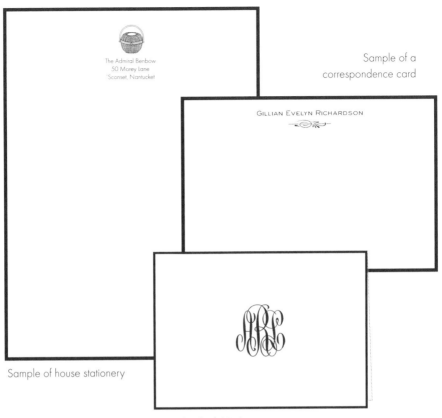

Sample of a
correspondence card

The Admiral Benbow
50 Morey Lane
'Sconset, Nantucket

GILLIAN EVELYN RICHARDSON

Sample of house stationery

Sample of a folded note

Correspondence cards are flat, heavy cards usually measuring $4\frac{1}{4}$" × $6\frac{1}{2}$" that are mailed in matching envelopes. They can be plain, bordered, or paneled, depending on one's tastes. A name, a small monogram, or motif may appear at the top of the card.

Traditionally, only the front of the card is written on, but as with folded notes, if you find the need to add a sentence or two, feel free to use the back.

HOUSE STATIONERY: House stationery may be properly used by any resident of your house or by any guest staying at your house. Many people keep house stationery at their country and beach homes so that stationery is always available for their guests and for themselves.

The name of your house or your address may appear on the stationery, or it can be illustrated with a line drawing of your house or an appropriate motif to illustrate the sense of the place.

· POINTS OF STYLE ·

Monograms and Names

Adding your name or monogram to stationery is a nice way to personalize your correspondence.

Thanks to an abundance of type styles and treatments there are numerous ways to create a personalization that best reflects you. Below are some traditional guidelines you may wish to consider when creating your personal look. But remember, these are only guidelines. Follow them or disregard as much as you need to create a design that best represents you.

MONOGRAMS: Married women use the initials that represent their given name, maiden surname, and married surname.

Single women, and married women who continue to use their maiden names, use the initials representing their given name, middle name, and surname.

Men use the initials that represent their given name, middle name, and surname.

When the letters in the monogram are the same size, the initials appear in order. If you choose a monogram style with a larger center initial, the initial representing your surname appears in the middle flanked by the initials of your given name on the left and your middle or maiden name on the right.

SAMPLES OF
MONOGRAMS FOR
BARBARA GREY NEWMAN

If a single initial is used, women use the first initial of their given name and men may use the first initial of their surname or given name.

NAMES: For the most formal social stationery, married women use their given name, maiden surname, and married surname. Single women and women who continue to use their maiden name use their full maiden name (given name, middle name, and maiden surname).

Men use their full names, without abbreviations or honorifics (Mr., Dr., Captain, etc.). If a man dislikes his middle name he may omit it entirely. For more casual correspondence, men and women should feel free to personalize their stationery as they would wish to be introduced at a social gathering. For example, a Maxwell Hopkins might prefer his stationery to simply read Max Hopkins.

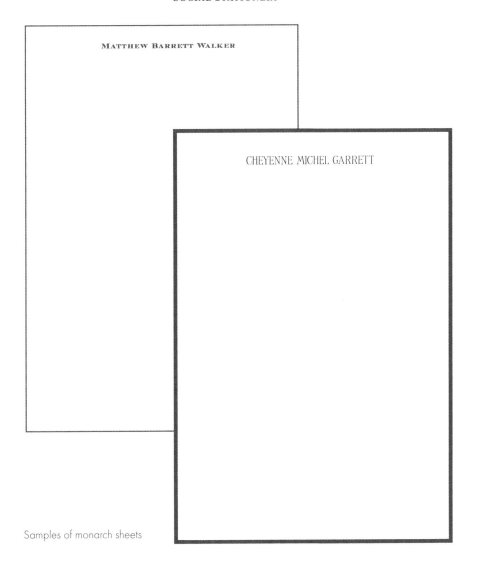

MATTHEW BARRETT WALKER

CHEYENNE MICHEL GARRETT

Samples of monarch sheets

SOCIAL STATIONERY FOR MEN

While the nature of your correspondence typically dictates the format, there's still plenty of flexibility in color, motif, and other design options.

For Letter Writing

MONARCH SHEETS: Most men use monarch sheets for personal correspondence and personal business letters. Monarch sheets, also known as "executive stationery," measure $7\frac{1}{4}"\times10\frac{1}{2}"$ and fold into thirds to fit their envelopes.

Although monarch sheets are available in a variety of colors, many men prefer ecru or white. Fashionable ink colors are also available but black, grey, and navy blue are the most popular.

Your name, address, or name and address may appear at the top of the sheets. The stationery retains a more personal look when you use only your name.

Only the front of the sheet is written on, never the back. If you need additional space, use blank second sheets.

CORRESPONDENCE SHEETS: Men who usually do not write long letters may prefer correspondence sheets to monarch sheets. Measuring $6^3/_8$" × $8^1/_2$", correspondence sheets are somewhat smaller than monarch sheets and fold in half to fit their envelopes. They may be embellished with your coat of arms, monogram, or with your name and address. Most men, however, prefer to print just their names.

Like monarch sheets, only the front of a correspondence sheet is written on, never the back. If you need additional space, use blank second sheets.

For Note Writing

CORRESPONDENCE CARDS: Correspondence cards are small, usually $4^1/_4$" × $6^1/_2$", heavy, flat cards that are used for thank-you notes and other brief notes. Men generally use these rather than fold-over notes. The cards are very practical and most men find that they use many more correspondence cards than sheets.

Your name (either full name or just your given name and surname), small monogram, or motif generally appears at the top. Using a monogram is the more social style. Using your name is a good option for personal notes and for notes to professional contacts. Some men have their name and address printed across the top of the card.

Traditionally, only the front of the card is written on, but as with folded notes, if you find the need to add a sentence or two, feel free to use the back.

ENVELOPES: Envelopes for social stationery are printed with your full address on the back flap. Your name is typically omitted. Traditionally, every word is spelled out. If you live in an apartment building, include your apartment number.

Samples of correspondence cards

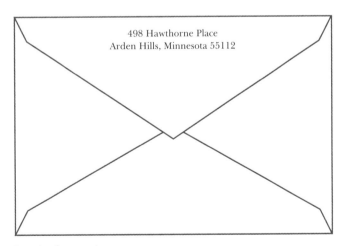

Sample of an envelope

The five- or nine-digit Zip Code, or complete Postal Code in Canada, should also be used on personal stationery.

HOUSE STATIONERY: House stationery may be properly used by any resident of your house or by any guest staying at your house. Many people keep house stationery at their country or beach homes so that stationery is always available for their guests and themselves.

House stationery typically features the name of the house or the address but can also be designed to fit the mood of the location. A graphic of a lake, a palm tree, or mountains are all nice ways to convey the feeling and spirit of the place.

POSTCARDS: Postcards are used for short, non-confidential correspondence. They are great for reminding people of "that" meeting. They can be printed with either your name or your name and address on one line at the top of the card. The maximum size that the Postal Service allows for reduced rate postage is $4\frac{1}{4}$" × 6".

CHAPTER TWO

Business and Professional Stationery

Each letter written on business stationery is a personal emissary from one office to another. Corporate stationery influences the impression formed in the mind of the recipient, not only about the individual sender, but also about the company he or she represents.

Several decisions need to be made when creating business and professional stationery. You'll need to consider the following points before selecting and designing your stationery.

1. What kind of paper should I use?
2. What items should I include in my corporate stationery wardrobe?
3. What information should I include?
4. What color ink should I use?
5. Should my stationery be engraved, thermographed, or flat-printed?

WHAT KIND OF PAPER SHOULD I USE?

Paper is made from either cotton or wood. The first true papers were made from cotton almost two thousand years ago. Wood-pulp papers came into being in the 1800s during the Industrial Revolution. In time, they replaced cotton-fiber papers for many uses because of their lower cost and the seemingly endless supply of trees from which to harvest wood pulp.

The finest paper, though, is made from cotton. Before you order your stationery, run your fingers across the paper. Stationery made from cotton will have a soft, rich feel. You will undoubtedly recognize its inherent quality. One hundred percent cotton fibers create the touch and feel of Crane's uncommonly beautiful papers.

Cotton papers are the ideal choice for stationery that is to be engraved or letterpressed. Because cotton fibers are soft and strong, they fully absorb and accept the deep impressions created through these printing processes. The inherent elegance and artistic qualities of both printing methods are truly best displayed and appreciated on 100% cotton paper.

Business papers come in a variety of colors. While white and ecru (also known as buff or cream) are the most formal, colors such as ivory, grey, and blue are frequently used as well, as today's color palette continues to expand.

WHAT COLOR INK SHOULD I USE?

While most businesses choose conservative ink colors such as black, navy, or grey, more and more businesses are using lively colors such as blue, red, green, gold, bronze, silver, and combinations of two or more colors. The correct colors for your business are the ones that best project your corporate identity and are appropriate for your field.

WHAT ITEMS SHOULD I INCLUDE IN MY CORPORATE STATIONERY WARDROBE?

There are many types of stationery that you might wish to include in your corporate stationery wardrobe. These items range from the basics, such as your corporate letterhead and business cards, to the more personal, such as correspondence cards and jotter cards. Many professionals start with the basics and add other items as their business grows or as their needs increase. This chapter discusses the many items that can make up a professional's stationery wardrobe.

WHAT TYPE OF PRINTING SHOULD I USE FOR MY STATIONERY?

Business and professional stationery can be engraved, blind-embossed, letterpressed, thermographed, lithographed, or even prepared on a quality office printer.

Engraving is one of the oldest and most beautiful processes for reproducing images on paper. The appeal of engraving lies in the exquisite detail created by its three-dimensional impression. Engraving is produced when the copy is etched in reverse into a copper plate. Ink is deposited in the resulting cavity. The engraving press then forces the paper into the cavity, creating a raised impression. The paper is literally raised with the ink adhering to the raised surface. The fact that the paper is raised is what distinguishes engraving from thermography and flat-printing.

It is easy to tell whether or not a piece of stationery is engraved. Simply turn it over. If there is an indentation (caused by the pressure from the engraving press), it is engraved. You can also tell by looking closely at the impression on the front. The paper will be smoother and there may be a little ripple to the sheet. This is called the "bruise" and is a natural part of the process.

Engraved stationery is more expensive than thermographed or printed stationery. However, much of the price difference lies in the initial cost of the engraving plate. Since engraving plates can be used over and over again, and since business stationery is often run in large quantities, the cost of engraved stationery is not necessarily much more expensive than thermographed or flat-printed stationery.

Blind-embossing (or just "embossing") is a process similar to engraving. A raised impression is created from a copper plate. But unlike engraving, no ink is used. Blind-embossing is commonly used for company logos on business cards and letterhead.

Letterpress began in Europe in the 14th century as an alternative to laborious calligraphy. It involves setting type in reverse on a letterpress plate, inking the plate, and then pressing it to the surface of the paper. The raised printing surfaces on the letterpress plate leave a deep impression on the paper. The depth of the image is accentuated by the ink and the minute shadows created within the impression. Letterpress offers a warmth and quality that is not easily duplicated by other printing methods.

Although sometimes called "raised printing," thermography is not raised at all. Unlike engraving where the paper is actually raised, the raise in thermography is created by a resinous powder that is melted over the flat-printed ink. Thermography is less expensive than engraving but not quite as appealing. Since it is less expensive, it might be chosen when smaller quantities are ordered, especially now that laser-friendly inks are available.

Lithography, also known as flat or offset printing, uses ink to print lettering or images onto paper. Lithography is the printing process most commonly used for mass-produced items such as posters, books, and newspapers. The finished product has a flat finish as opposed to the raised or indented finishes of engraved items.

A top-of-the-line home or office printer is also a viable option for creating personalized stationery. At-home or -office printing is a cost-effective way to make multiple versions of stationery that represent different divisions of a company in small quantities. It's particularly ideal for businesses that will need to update their contact information due to a change of mailing or web address. While at-home or -office printing cannot match the look and feel of engraving, when done well, it can be an appropriate option for business and professional correspondence.

WHAT INFORMATION SHOULD I INCLUDE?

Include your company's name, address, phone number, fax number, and your website. If the stationery is to be personalized, add your name, title, and other ways you welcome contact such as your email address or cellular phone number.

CREATING YOUR BUSINESS
STATIONERY WARDROBE

When most people think of business stationery they naturally think of corporate letterhead. While useful for formal communication, standard letterhead isn't appropriate for all types of correspondence. A well-rounded stationery wardrobe will include items suited for both formal and informal communication.

Corporate Letterhead

This 8½" × 11" sheet is the basic stationery used by most businesses. It is used not only to communicate, but also to project a corporate image. Information on the letterhead may include the firm's name, address, phone number, fax number, and website. It may also include an executive or partner's name, title, email address, and cellular phone number. Because there can be so much information on the letterhead, many companies are placing some of the information on a line running across the bottom of the page.

Enfield &
Regala ATTORNEYS AT LAW

55 State Street
Boston, Massachusetts 02110

www.enfieldregala.com

SENIOR COUNSEL
Chris Doherty
Ashkley Ohrenstein

OF COUNSEL
Gordon Eric Rumley
Dave Ratzlaff
William Sche

ASSOCIATES
Wendy Soley
David Quinn
Allison Torvi
Randy Armst
Cristal Han

BISHOP & YORK

BISHOP & YORK

CERTIFIED PUBLIC ACCOUNTANTS

295 COTTAGE COURT
MONTAUK, NEW YORK 11954

CERTIFIED PUBLIC ACCOUNTANTS

295 COTTAGE COURT, MONTAUK, NEW YORK 11954
TELEPHONE 631-555-1212 FACSIMILE 631-555-2121 WWW.BISHOPYORK.COM

Samples of corporate letterhead

Most members of a firm use the universal letterhead displaying the corporate identity and the basic information, such as the address and phone number. Partners and senior executives, however, generally use the same letterhead with their name, title, and, perhaps, other pertinent information added.

The company name and address appear on the envelope's front top left corner or, less frequently, centered on the back flap. The standard business envelope is $9\frac{1}{2}"\times 4\frac{1}{8}"$.

Monarch Sheets

Monarch sheets or executive stationery ($7\frac{1}{4}"\times 10\frac{1}{2}"$) are slightly smaller and, therefore, more personal than the standard $8\frac{1}{2}"\times 11"$ sheets. Monarch sheets can be used as business letterhead or for personal business letters. They are especially appropriate as letterhead in businesses where a personal touch might be helpful, perhaps by designers, consultants, or executives of small businesses. When used as letterhead, they display the same information found on a standard $8\frac{1}{2}"\times 11"$ sheet. Since monarch sheets are smaller, you might want to have only essential information printed.

Personal business letters, mentioned in the last paragraph, are letters sent on behalf of the business to an individual with whom you are on a first-name basis. They display only the executive's name at the top of the sheet. The company name and address appear on the back flap of the envelope.

Correspondence Cards

Many business occasions and meetings call for a brief thank-you or congratulatory note to be sent. Correspondence cards are the perfect stationery product to meet these needs. They are flat, heavy cards ($4\frac{1}{4}"\times 6\frac{1}{4}"$) that are used to send brief, handwritten notes. A note on a correspondence card is effective in a way an email message or phone call cannot match. It is a tangible and personal way to demonstrate your interest in nurturing the business relationship.

Your name generally appears at the top of your correspondence cards. Your company's name and address appear on the back flap of the envelope. An emerging trend today finds businesses—especially entrepreneurs—using correspondence cards as their main format for written communication.

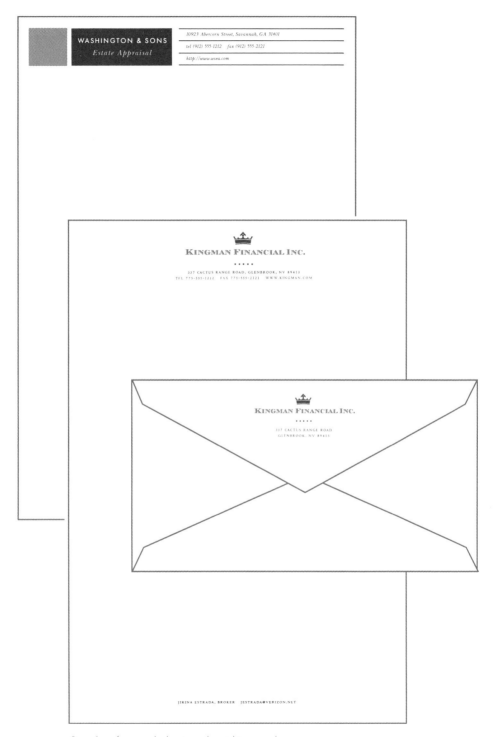

WASHINGTON & SONS
Estate Appraisal

10923 Abercorn Street, Savannah, GA 31401

tel (912) 555-1212   fax (912) 555-2121

http://www.wsea.com

KINGMAN FINANCIAL INC.

337 CACTUS RANGE ROAD, GLENBROOK, NV 89413
TEL 775-555-1212   FAX 775-555-2121   WWW.KINGMAN.COM

KINGMAN FINANCIAL INC.

337 CACTUS RANGE ROAD
GLENBROOK, NV 89413

JIRINA ESTRADA, BROKER   JESTRADA@VERIZON.NET

Samples of monarch sheets and matching envelope

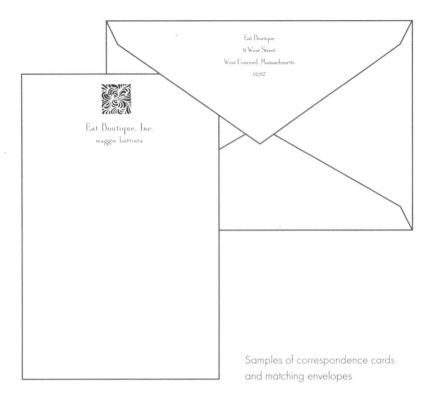

Eat Boutique
9 West Street
West Concord, Massachusetts
01267

Eat Boutique, Inc.
maggie battista

Samples of correspondence cards
and matching envelopes

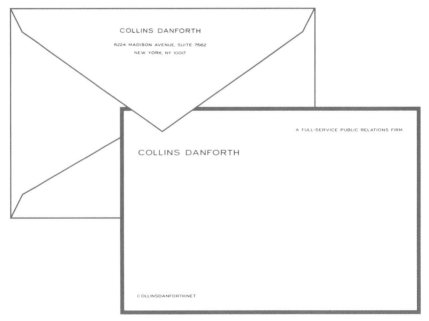

COLLINS DANFORTH
6224 MADISON AVENUE, SUITE 7562
NEW YORK, NY 10017

A FULL-SERVICE PUBLIC RELATIONS FIRM

COLLINS DANFORTH

COLLINSDANFORTH.NET

Business Cards

Business cards provide clients or potential clients with all the information they need to contact you. Cards should list the pertinent information neatly and concisely. Remember, a card is a communication tool, not an advertisement. Including a list of services or products reduces the card's formality. Information should include your name and title, company name, mailing and/or street addresses, phone number, cellular phone number, fax number, email address, and even your company's web address.

A 3½" × 2" card (horizontal) is the standard in business in the United States. A 2" × 3½" card (vertical) is frequently used by professionals in the creative fields, as are other sizes such as 3½" × 2½". Formal business cards are printed only on one side, except for bilingual cards that are in one language on one side and in a second language on the reverse.

The most formal business cards are white or ecru and printed in black or grey ink, but cards can be printed on any colored stock using virtually any color ink including metallics. In some instances, multiple ink colors are used to reflect a corporate identity.

Samples of business cards

· POINTS OF STYLE ·

Business Card Protocol

The quality and appearance of your business card says a great deal about you and your company. So does the manner in which you distribute them. Here are a few points to keep in mind regarding use of your cards:

Present your card with the print facing the recipient so they can read it when presented.

Don't give out a business card that is defective, out of date, or soiled. Carry cards in a card case to keep them fresh and protected.

Don't pass out your cards like flyers to a shoe sale. Handing your card out indiscriminately will make you appear pushy and unprofessional.

When receiving a card, take time to look at it as it is representative of the person and his or her business and may help you remember his or her name in the future.

Social Business Cards

Business cards are not generally exchanged during social occasions or in social situations. However, a practical solution to missing a networking opportunity is to have a social business card that can be exchanged.

Traditionally, social business cards are the same size as a standard business card and are produced on white or ecru stock with black or grey ink. However, it's increasingly common for cards, particularly those used by those in creative fields, to be produced in square, fold-over, and even die-cut formats in a wide range of colors.

Cards should be imprinted with your name, office phone number, and other ways you welcome business contacts such as your cellular phone number and email address. They do not include your company information, your title, or a mailing address.

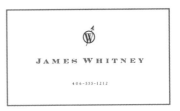

Sample of a social business card

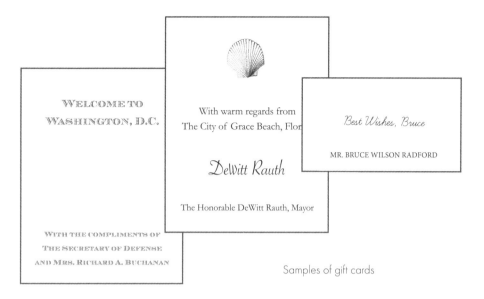

Samples of gift cards

Gift Cards

Gift cards are placed inside the box of a business gift. The signature of the presenter may be preprinted on the card, or the card may be designed to be individually hand signed. Size will vary depending on the amount of information needed on the card. Sizes such as $3\frac{1}{2}$" × 2" or 5" × $3\frac{1}{2}$" are typical.

"With Compliments" Cards

A "With Compliments" card, typically $3\frac{1}{2}$" × $6\frac{3}{4}$", is attached to an item of interest, such as a magazine or annual report, when it is forwarded. It folds so when attached to the item, the "With Compliments" or "For Your Interest" is visible.

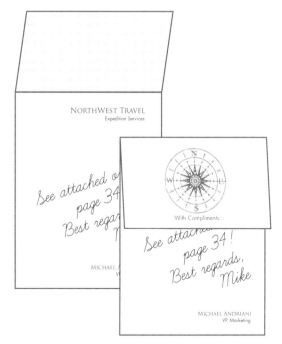

Sample of "with compliments" card, opened and closed.

Memo Pads

Memo pads (5" × 7") can be used to jot down notes during meetings and phone calls. Your name and, if you choose, your title appear at the top of each sheet.

Jotter Cards

Jotter cards are 3" × 5" cards on which your name or name, address, and phone number appear at the top. Jotter cards are typically kept inside a leather carrying case and are ideal for meetings and trade shows. Jotters can also be kept readily available on your desk in an open-top holder. Their extra space affords you the opportunity to jot down a reminder to your clients as to why they might want to get in touch with you on a specific matter.

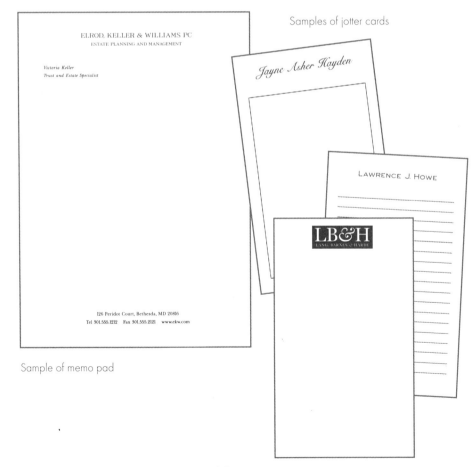

Samples of jotter cards

Sample of memo pad

CORRESPONDENCE RELATED TO EMPLOYMENT

Your résumé and letter of application are the first impression a potential employer has of you. It's worth your time and effort to present yourself clearly and professionally.

RÉSUMÉS: With today's electronic style of submitting résumés and applications, a great way to "outclass the competition" is to submit or follow up an electronic version with a traditional résumé on fine stationery. Like corporate letterhead, résumé stationery is $8\frac{1}{2}" \times 11"$ in size and comes in various weights and

---

ZOEY CATHERINE RAUTH
12 Highland Avenue
Bryn Mawr, PA 19010
555 774-1754 | zoey@nomaila.com

OBJECTIVE: To gain experience as a copy editor, as a first step toward a career in publishing.

EDUCATION: *B.A. in literature, 2008*
Bennington College, Bennington, VT

Courses in contemporary and classic literature, creative writing, history of the English language, and screenwriting.

Academic scholarships, 2005-2008. Contributor, *Silo*, a student-created and -designed journal of art, writing, and music, 2006-2008. Staff member *Bennington Free Press*, 2006-2008. Maple Sugaring Project, 2006.

EXPERIENCE: *Editorial Assistant, VermontTiger.com, Field Work Term 2007-2008*
Responsible for fact-checking, proofreading, and copy editing prior to daily postings. Prepared press releases and responses to reader letters and queries. Maintained editorial database of archived copy.

Administrative Assistant, WHYY, Philadelphia, PA, May-August 2006
Assisted with scheduling and creation of underwriter spots. Prepared copy for fund drive messaging used both on-air and on station website. Proofread all outgoing marketing materials. Performed various secretarial tasks including composition and distribution of memos and recording minutes at meetings. Solicited contributions for fund drives.

SKILLS: Excellent communication skills in writing, over the phone, and face to face. Proven ability to work under deadlines and handle multiple tasks simultaneously. Ability to master or create new systems efficiently. Mastery of Microsoft Office, Quark, and HTML.

Sample of a résumé

conservative colors. When you mail a résumé, you should always include an application cover letter. Your cover letter and envelope should match your résumé stationery in color, font style, and size, and should be hand addressed.

FOLLOW-UP LETTERS: A follow-up letter is sent immediately after an interview. It is used to thank the interviewer for spending time with you, giving you insight into the available position and the organization, and for considering your qualifications for the position.

ACCEPTANCE LETTERS: The easiest letter and most pleasant to write! Used to accept the job, confirm details of your working arrangements, such as starting date, and to express pleasure in coming to work for the organization and the person who has offered you the job.

Jeremy Thomas
119 Copper Circle
Little Rock, AR 72206
Phone: 501-555-3646 • E-mail: Jthomas@aol.com

August 15, 2008

Mrs. Patricia Cameron
Director of Human Resources
Lohan & Lohan
11875 Brennan Court
Dallas, TX 75202

Dear Mrs. Cameron:

I am writing to apply for the programmer position advertised in the *Dallas IT Journal*. As specified in the ad, I am enclosing my résumé, my certification, and three references. I believe my extensive technical experience and education make me an excellent candidate for the position. As the following comparison shows, I possess many of the skills required for the role:

Your Requirements	My Qualifications
College degree	B.S. degree in Computer Programming
Web-based applications experience	6 years experience using Java language and application server
Language skills	Competent in JSP, SQL, HTML

The enclosed résumé provides additional information about my work experience.

I would welcome the opportunity to meet with you and discuss the opportunity further. I will call your office on August 24 to schedule a meeting at your convenience.

Sincerely,

Jeremy Thomas

Jeremy Thomas

Sample format for a cover letter

CHAPTER THREE

Business and Professional Invitations

BUSINESS INVITATIONS

Business invitations may be created for any type of corporate function from a grand opening or relocation of offices to a reception honoring a retiree or a top salesperson. They may be formal or informal, depending on the purpose of the event and the impression you want to create. Many times, a corporate logo is placed at the top of the invitation.

While it is impossible to include every type of invitation that you might use, almost any situation can be handled by looking at the samples provided and substituting your information. For example, if your company, the XYZ Company, were hosting a dinner to honor the accomplishments of your senior editor, you might use the format on the following page, substituting your company's name on the invitation line, dinner for reception on Event Line 1, "in honor of" on Event Line 2, and your senior editor's name on Event Line 3.

By following this format, you can create copy for any type of invitation for any event. You can even start with this format and change the order in which the information is presented. The important thing is simply to make sure that all of the necessary information is included. See both sample #1 and sample #2 on the next page.

SAMPLE #1:

Invitation Line	Mr. Herbert Sanders
Request Line	requests the pleasure of your company
Event Line #1	at a reception
Event Line #2	to introduce the 2009 Holiday Line from
Event Line #3	Sharon Jay Togs
Date Line	Thursday, the fifth of April
Time Line	at seven o'clock
Location Line	The Red Lion Inn
Address Line	30 Main Street
City and State Line	Stockbridge, Massachusetts 01262
Reply Request Line	Please reply

SAMPLE #2:

Event Line #2	To introduce the 2009 Holiday Line from
Event Line #3	Sharon Jay Togs
Invitation Line	Mr. Herbert Sanders
Request Line	requests the pleasure of your company
Event Line #1	at a reception
Date Line	Thursday, the third of April
Time Line	at seven o'clock
Location Line	The Red Lion Inn
Address Line	30 Main Street
City and State Line	Stockbridge, Massachusetts 01262
Reply Request Line	Please reply

As you can see, all of the information is the same. It is just presented in a different sequence.

Reply Request Line on Business Invitations

On business invitations, there are many options to request your guest's reply. Telephone or email replies are perfectly acceptable and they are the most effective in gathering timely and accurate information. R.S.V.P., R.s.v.p., RSVP, and Rsvp are all forms of acceptable abbreviations.

R.s.v.p. by January 15, 2009

Ms. Jeane Anderson at (888) 123-4567

or email jeane.anderson@acme.org

Additional Specific Instructions

Other specific instructions can be added below the Reply Request Line, on the lower right-hand corner, across from the Reply Request information, or on a separate card. "Special Instructions" could provide information on how to dress such as "Business Attire," or details of the event such as "Invitation is not transferable," "Please present invitation at the door," or "This invitation admits two."

OFFICIAL INVITATIONS

Official invitations differ from business invitations by the host of the event being an elected or appointed official such as a U.S. governor, Secretary of State, or mayor of a city.

SAMPLE #1: INVITATION TO CELEBRATE

Mr. Bruce Wilson Radford

Representative from Illinois

requests the pleasure of your company

at dinner

to honor the

Seventy-fifth Anniversary

of the

Public Utilities Forum

Saturday, the sixteenth of January

Two thousand and ten

at seven o'clock

Frist Center for Visual Arts

919 Broadway

Nashville, Tennessee

R.s.v.p. (615) 234-5678

Ms. Anne Parker

Business Attire

SAMPLE #2: INVITATIONS TO HONOR

In Honor of
Mr. Paul James Travis
Superintendent of the Oak Brook School District

Mr. Bruce Wilson Radford
Mayor of Oak Brook
requests the pleasure of your company
at a reception
Wednesday, the fourth of March
Two thousand and nine
at six o'clock
Hyatt Lodge
McDonalds Campus

R.s.v.p.   2815 Jorie Boulevard
(630) 234-5678   Oak Brook, Illinois

Note: You doubly distinguish your honored guest when you list his or her
name at the top of the invitation.

• POINTS OF STYLE •

Grammar and Company Names

A rule of thumb: The name of a company is a singular entity that requires the
use of a singular verb. For example:

Simpson, Healy Investments, Inc. announces that its offices

or

Adamson and Shelton is pleased to announce

BUSINESS ANNOUNCEMENTS

Business announcements are sent to inform clients of a change in the status of a company. Announcements may be sent for any number of reasons, the most popular being a change of address, change of partners, introduction of a new officer, or even the introduction of a new product.

Business announcements are generally conservative unless the nature of your business allows for a flourish of creativity. As such, they are generally engraved in black ink on ecru or white card stock.

There are many choices of lettering styles from which to choose. Roman and block styles are the most popular for formal business announcements. More decorative and cursive styles lend a more social look to your announcement (for sample type styles, see page 34).

Opening an office

JOHN EVAN KAUFMAN, D.D.S.

ANNOUNCES THE OPENING OF HIS OFFICE

FOR THE

GENERAL PRACTICE OF DENTISTRY

PREVENTIVE · RESTORATIVE · COSMETIC

305 DEL MONTE BOULEVARD

SAN FRANCISCO, CALIFORNIA 94112

FOR APPOINTMENTS
(415) 555-1212

OFFICE HOURS
MONDAY - FRIDAY
8:00 - 4:00

HOUGHTON, WELMSLEY & HOWE

ANNOUNCES THAT ITS LAW OFFICE

IS NOW LOCATED AT

56 OMEGA AVENUE

PROVIDENCE, RHODE ISLAND 02903

(410) 555-1212

Relocating an office

Green&Hart

Green&Hart Investment Group
is pleased to announce that
Elizabeth Stokes Lindenman
has joined the company as
Vice President

65 Financial Place
New York, NY 10005

Admittance of a new associate

It is with sadness that we
announce the death of
Jonathan Lewis Vorhees
Editor in Chief
November twenty-second
Two thousand and two

McCullough Publishing Company

Announcement
of a death

Brian R. Toomey
and
Henry T. Warren
announce the formation of a partnership
for the general practice of law
under the firm name of
Toomey and Warren

725 Rio Grande Boulevard, N.W.
Albuquerque, New Mexico 87104

Formation of a partnership

Adamson and Shelton
Attorneys at Law
is pleased to announce that
David S. Clifford
has been admitted to the partnership
The firm will now be known as
Adamson, Shelton and Clifford

1300 Walnut Street
Philadelphia, Pennsylvania 19107   (215) 555-1212

Admittance of a
new partner

CHAPTER FOUR

Wedding Invitations and Announcements

Congratulations on your pending union. This is no doubt a very busy and exciting time filled with emotion and plenty of decision-making. The fact that you are reading this means you are concerned with making sure every detail is attended to properly. We applaud you for that. And we also offer this bit of good news: the rules surrounding wedding stationery etiquette are no longer etched in stone. Today's couple has more room than ever to stretch and bend some long-standing rules to suit their particular circumstances.

As our society evolves, so does our etiquette. The fact that people are marrying later, the emergence of interfaith marriages, second and third weddings, and alternative ceremonies all contribute to the changing rules of etiquette. Many of the rules of etiquette were made (and continue to be made) to deal with changing social situations. Some of the etiquette deemed proper today would have been unthinkable generations ago. And, surely, a generation from now many of the guidelines presented here will seem archaic.

When all is said and done, etiquette is based on common sense and courtesy. Your guests need certain information to get them to your wedding—the date, the time, and the location. You of course want to convey this as graciously as possible while injecting a bit of your own personality and a sense of the event into your wedding correspondence.

While the text that follows offers information on the basic etiquette surrounding wedding invitations and stationery, it is meant only as a guideline. As such, the information contained in these pages is meant to help direct, not dictate, how you choose to handle this most personal and important correspondence. Take what information you need to make your invitation work for you and don't worry about what you leave behind.

In the same way that no two couples, unions, or families are alike, no two invitation ensembles will ever be either. What's most important is that your invitation expresses your joy, invites your friends and loved ones to come celebrate, and marks the beginning of a new chapter in your life.

SELECTING YOUR WEDDING INVITATION

Wedding invitations set the tone for the wedding. If you haven't sent a save-the-date, the invitation is the first exposure people will have to your wedding and will create your guests' first impressions. Not only do your invitations tell them where and when your wedding is being held, they subtly tell them how formal it is and how they should dress.

When you select your wedding invitations, keep in mind what kind of wedding you are having. Your invitations and your wedding should complement one another. While formal invitations are appropriate for, among other things, a traditional church wedding, something less formal and more colorful may be a better choice for a wedding held at sunset on a beach.

Wedding invitations should be ordered at least three months before your wedding. This should leave you enough time for producing your invitations and addressing and mailing them. (Wedding invitations should be mailed four to six weeks before the wedding.) Of course, it is best to order them as soon as you have all the necessary information.

WHERE TO PURCHASE YOUR
WEDDING INVITATION

Many places sell wedding invitations including stationery stores, engravers, department stores, and specialty or online stores. When selecting a stationer, you should look for one who has expertise in selling wedding invitations and with whom you feel comfortable working. A quality stationer will be a valuable resource and not just an order taker. Your stationer should be able to understand and interpret your vision for your invitation and offer ideas and guidance on its design. He or she should be able to answer or find the answer to any questions regarding types of printing, paper stock, the components of your invitation and wedding set, and timing for mailing. He or she should also be able to address issues of etiquette and wording for your invitation.

If, after a first meeting, you're not comfortable with a stationer's competencies in these areas, keep looking. You don't want to risk disappointment on any element of your wedding stationery.

Invitation costs will vary as they are determined by the quality of the invitation, the number of enclosures, and the quantity ordered. When selecting your invitations, it is important to remember that even though the invitations set the tone for the entire wedding, they comprise, on average, only about two percent of the cost of the wedding. No matter how much money you save by purchasing inexpensive invitations, it will be a tiny amount in relation to the overall cost of your wedding.

CHOOSING A PAPER FOR YOUR WEDDING INVITATION

Your wedding papers will most likely be made from either cotton or wood. The first true papers were made from cotton almost two thousand years ago. Wood-pulp papers came into being in the 1800s during the Industrial Revolution. They supplanted cotton-fiber papers for many uses because of their lower cost and the seemingly endless supply of trees.

Cotton papers are the ideal choice for invitations that are to be engraved or letterpressed. Because cotton fibers are soft and strong, they fully absorb and accept deep impressions created through these printing processes. The inherent qualities of both printing methods are truly best displayed and appreciated on 100% cotton paper.

CHOOSING A FORMAT FOR YOUR WEDDING INVITATION

A well-chosen wedding invitation reflects the character of the individuals being joined and the nature of the ceremony planned. In much the same way that no couple is alike, no two wedding invitations need ever be alike either. Today brides and grooms have a virtually limitless selection of formats to choose from and can even create their own. While traditional styles are typically more formal and are always appropriate, those same styles can be easily updated to express your values while presenting a touch of personality.

The most traditional invitation format has a fold on the left-hand side and opens like a book. This type of stationery is called a wedding sheet. The invitation may be either plain or paneled. Paneled invitations have a blind-embossed frame. The decision on which one to choose is usually determined by the lettering style selected.

Another traditional-style invitation is a heavyweight flat card. It can be as simple as an ecru or white card, to those incorporating a panel, hand bordering, or beveled edges with hand-applied gold or silver leaf. It's also not uncommon to see couples add their own flair to this traditional style by using a colored stock with a colored ink and even embellishing it with a somewhat casual motif.

No matter which format you choose, you should always ask to see a proof so you can see what the invitation will look like before it goes to press. While some script lettering styles can look beautiful on a sample invitation, they may need to be condensed or expanded to fit the format of your invitation and consequently not look the way you anticipated. A proof eliminates surprises and is a small, wise investment.

CHOOSING A SIZE

While in the past there were traditional sizes for invitations, today's couples are bound only by their imagination when choosing a size for their invitation. When designing your invitation, make sure there is an appropriate-size envelope for the invitation and all the components. You should also be aware that any over- or off-size invitations may require extra postage.

CHOOSING A PAPER COLOR

Formal wedding invitations are traditionally engraved on either ecru or white stationery. Ecru is the color you may know as buff, cream, ivory, or eggshell. It is the off-white color that is typically associated with wedding invitations. Ecru is the more popular traditional choice in the Americas while white is the color of choice in Europe.

However, invitations can be produced on literally any color paper. In fact it's quite common for a couple to choose an invitation that reflects the overall color scheme of their wedding. The color that you choose is first and foremost a matter of personal preference.

Mr. and Mrs. David Leyton Jones

request the honour of your presence

at the marriage of their daughter

Bronwyn Alice

to

Mr. Andrew Philip Smallwood

Saturday, the fifth of June

two thousand ten

at half after eleven o'clock

Brandywine Valley Baptist Church

Wilmington, Delaware

Samples of wedding invitations

DR. AND MRS. ADAM NAUGHTON

REQUEST THE HONOR OF YOUR COMPANY

AT THE MARRIAGE OF THEIR DAUGHTER

Kelly Ann

TO

Michael Plimpton

SATURDAY, THE THIRTEENTH OF JUNE

TWO THOUSAND TEN

AT FOUR O'CLOCK IN THE AFTERNOON

WAVE HILL

BRONX, NEW YORK

Reception immediately following

LEEZA
FARELLA OTTAVIO
GIANNINI

request the pleasure of your company

at their wedding and celebration

Saturday, the eighth of May

Two thousand ten

at six o'clock in the evening

56 Kensington Parkway

Kansas City, Missouri

CHOOSING A LETTERING STYLE

Selecting a lettering style can be a challenging and confusing task. While helpful, style charts present just one line of each particular style surrounded by a myriad of other styles. They do not give you a very good idea of how the whole invitation will look. One of the best ways to choose a lettering style is to look at sample invitations. Your stationer should have an ample supply for you to review. This allows you to see what your invitations will look like in each lettering style. Be sure to focus on how the specific letters appear, especially those in your name. With some script typefaces, a capital "S" may look more like a "J." A letter-by-letter review will help you avoid any unwanted surprises.

But whether your invitation is traditional or not, the lettering style you choose should reflect the tone of your wedding and your personal taste.

CHOOSING AN INK COLOR

While black ink remains the most formal and popular ink color, there really are no hard and fast rules when it comes to the color of ink on your invitation. Your own personal design aesthetic and legibility should guide you in your selection.

Many couples choose a color that reflects the season or tone of the event or one that coordinates with the color palette of the wedding.

The printing process, as well as the color of the paper you choose, will also impact your ink color selection. For example, an engraved metallic monogram or motif will have a jewel-like quality to it that cannot be matched by any other printing process. To avoid any unwelcome surprises, ask your stationer to provide you examples of your ink and paper choice produced with the method you will be using for your invitation.

CHOOSING A METHOD OF PRINTING

Today there are more printing options for wedding invitations than ever. Each method offers its own advantages, ranging from quality to convenience, and lends its own sense of style to each piece of stationery you create.

Engraving

Engraving is one of the oldest and most beautiful processes for reproducing images on paper. It was developed during the 1500s and was initially used to

A SAMPLING
OF WEDDING TYPESTYLES

mr. and mrs. andrew jay forrester
ASHLYN

Mr. and Mrs. Andrew Jay Forrester
BASKERVILLE ROMAN ITALIC

Mr. and Mrs. Andrew Jay Forrester
BERNHARD FASHION

Mr. and Mrs. Andrew Jay Forrester
BICKHAM SCRIPT

MR. AND MRS. ANDREW JAY FORRESTER
CENTAUR

MR. AND MRS. ANDREW JAY FORRESTER
COPPERPLATE

Mr. and Mrs. Andrew Jay Forrester
FINEHAND

MR. AND MRS. ANDREW JAY FORRESTER
HANNA

Mr. and Mrs. Andrew Jay Forrester
STATESMAN

reproduce the documents and announcements that were at that time copied by hand. The appeal of engraving is in the exquisite detail created by its three-dimensional impression.

Engravers were talented craftsmen who carried their trade from the Old World to the Americas. Their craft was not only used to produce stationery and announcements but also currency papers, such as stocks, bonds, and dollar bills. Perhaps the United States' most famous engraver was Paul Revere.

The most elegant invitations are still engraved. It has a warmth all its own that conveys an unspoken message of distinction and timelessness. The first step in creating such a truly unique invitation is to transfer the image, or text, to a copper plate. The invitation copy is etched in reverse into a copper plate. Ink is deposited into the resulting cavity. The engraving press then forces the paper into the cavity, creating a raised impression. The paper is literally raised with the ink adhering to its surface. This is the process that creates the sharp definition that is associated with the engraving art.

Every engraved invitation is fed into the engraving press by hand. The press is adjusted to accommodate the specific typestyle, paper, and type selected by the customer. For certain types of metallic inks, an additional pass through the engraving press is required to "burnish" the image and to bring out the richness of the ink's tone. Because there is no mass production in engraving, each impression, each invitation, is a customized one.

Blind-embossing

Blind-embossing (or just "embossing") is a process similar to engraving. As with engraving, a raised impression is created from a copper plate. Unlike engraving, no ink is used. Blind-embossing is commonly used for a family coat of arms, the return address on the outside envelopes, and monograms. Dies made for blind-embossing can be used again to blind-emboss. They cannot, however, be used for engraving with ink.

Letterpress

Letterpress began in Europe in the 14th century as an alternative to laborious calligraphy. Type was hand-cast and individual characters were hand-set into lines until machine-set composition made the process easier. Today, many designers are returning to the craft of letterpress as a unique option to other printing methods.

Often used in combination with soft, handmade papers, the raised printing surfaces on a letterpress plate leave a deep impression on the paper. The depth of the image is accentuated by the ink and minute shadows created within the impression. Letterpress offers a warmth and quality that is not easily duplicated by other printing methods.

Thermography

Thermography is sometimes called "raised printing." Unlike engraving, where the paper is actually raised, the raise in thermography is created by a resinous powder that is melted over the flat-printed ink. Thermography is less expensive than engraving and can give your invitations a look similar to but not quite as nice as engraving. The letters on a thermographed invitation will have a shiny appearance.

Lithography

Also referred to as flat or offset printing, lithography uses ink to print lettering or images but does not yield a raised or indented appearance. Lithography is the most affordable printing option.

COMPOSING YOUR WEDDING INVITATION

The traditional wedding invitation has changed little throughout the years. Its essential purpose is to invite your guests and to tell them where and when your wedding is being held. It is that simplicity, coupled with fine paper and handsome design, that makes formal wedding invitations so elegant.

There are a number of basic points of etiquette that should be followed when wording a traditional wedding invitation. The following section covers the correct wording line by line and touches on other elements that a couple may choose to include on their invitation.

Host Line

Wedding invitations are properly issued by the parents of the bride. This tradition and the tradition of the bride's father giving away the bride have their origins in the days when the bride's father made the marriage arrangements for his daughter by negotiating the size of her dowry. Today, the traditions continue with the bride's family customarily hosting the wedding. Assuming the bride's parents are still married, their names appear on the first line of the wedding invitations.

If the bride's parents are divorced, the parents' names appear on separate lines with the mother's name always appearing first. The word "and" is not used to join them.

For more information on wording for divorced parents, see page 50.

Mr. and Mrs. Andrew Jay Forrester

request the honour of your presence

at the marriage of their daughter

Jennifer Marie

etc.

Bride's Father Holds a Doctorate

The use of "Doctor" on a formal invitation is always used for medical doctors and clergy with advanced degrees. Those holding doctorates in academia or research positions may or may not use "Doctor" socially: check for their personal preference. When the bride's father uses "Doctor" both professionally and socially, "Doctor" is written out, but may be abbreviated if he has an unusually long name.

Doctor and Mrs. Alexander Buchanan Westerhaven

Dr. and Mrs. Alexander Buchanan Westerhaven

Bride's Mother Holds a Doctorate

Traditionally, the bride's mother uses her social name—"Mrs." (husband's full name)—so the Invitational Line reads "Mr. and Mrs. Paul James Purcell."

However, today almost every woman holding a medical degree and many holding doctorates and working in academia or research use "Dr." both professionally and socially. If this is the mother's preference, display the mother's name on the first line of the invitation and her husband's name on

Mr. and Mrs. Andrew Jay Forrester — host line

request the honour of your presence

at the marriage of their daughter — request lines

Jennifer Marie — bride's name

to — joining word

Mr. Nicholas Jude Strickland — groom's name

Saturday, the twenty-first of August — date line

Two thousand and ten — year line

at six o'clock — time line

Church of Christ — location

1223 Roaring Brook Road — address

Bedford, New York — city and state

the second line preceded by the word "and." Use of "and" indicates they are married.

Dr. Laura Simpson Purcell

and Mr. Paul James Purcell

Bride's Father Is Clergy

While certain very high clergy may have special forms of address, most Christian ministers, priests, or pastors are addressed with the courtesy title "The Reverend".

"The Reverend" is not combined with another honorific and should immediately precede a full name. While a protestant minister with a doctorate is orally addressed as "Dr. (surname)", in writing he or she is correctly addressed as "The Reverend (full name)". "The Reverend Doctor (full name)" should be avoided unless you know it to be his or her personal preference.

If the bride's father is a rabbi, the names should read:

Rabbi and Mrs. Joshua Zev Allan

Bride's Mother Is Clergy

Display the mother's name on the first line of the invitation and her husband's name on the second line preceded by the word "and." The use of "and" indicates they are married.

The Reverend Laura Simpson Purcell

and Mr. Paul James Purcell

If the bride's mother is a rabbi, the parents' names should read:

Rabbi Lisa Stein Allan

and Mr. Joshua Zev Allan

Both Parents Are Clergy

If both parents are addressed as "The Reverend" their names should read:

The Reverend Laura Simpson Purcell

and The Reverend Paul James Purcell

If both the bride's parents are rabbis their names should read:

Rabbi Lisa Stein Allan

and Rabbi Joshua Zev Allan

"The Reverends Purcell" and "The Rabbis Allan" are also acceptable, but are less formal. Use of "and" indicates they are married.

Bride's Father Addressed as "the Honorable"

If the bride's father is a judge, an elected official, or was appointed to a very high office by the president of the United States, he is formally addressed as "the Honorable (full name)" for life. But "the Honorable" is not used when issuing an invitation: "the Honorable" is bestowed by others and never used by the person himself.

If the father holds, or has held, an office that grants use of a special honorific such as "Judge" or "Senator," use the honorific of the office.

Judge and Mrs. Paul James Purcell

If the father holds, or has held, an office granting address as "the Honorable" but has no special honorific such as "Judge" or "Senator," use "Mr." on the Invitational Line.

Mr. and Mrs. Paul James Purcell

Bride's Mother Addressed as "the Honorable"

If the bride's mother is a judge, an elected official, or was appointed to a very high office by the president of the United States, she is formally addressed as "the Honorable (full name)" for life. But "the Honorable" is not used when issuing an invitation: "the Honorable" is bestowed by others and never used by the person herself.

If the mother holds, or has held, an office that grants use of a special honorific such as "Judge" or "Senator," use the honorific of the office. Display the mother's name on the first line and her husband's on the second line preceded by the word "and." Use of "and" indicates they are married.

Judge Laura Simpson Purcell

and Mr. Paul James Purcell

If the mother holds, or has held, an office granting address as "the Honorable" but has no special honorific such as "Judge" or "Senator," use the standard "Mr. and Mrs." on the Invitational Line.

Mr. and Mrs. Paul James Purcell

Both Parents Are Addressed as "The Honorable"

"The Honorable" is not used on the Invitational Line.

If a parent holds a high office that grants use of a special honorific such as "Judge" or "Senator," use the honorific of his or her office before his or her name. If a parent holds a high office without a special honorific, use the standard "Mr." or "Mrs." with his or her name.

Display the holder of the higher office on the top line, the holder of the lower office on the second line, preceded by the word "and" to indicate they are married. If they hold offices of equal rank, display the mother's name on the first line and her husband's name on the second line preceded by the word "and."

Judge Laura Simpson Purcell

and Mr. Paul James Purcell

Judge Paul James Purcell
and Mrs. Purcell

Judge Laura Simpson Purcell
and Judge Paul James Purcell

Parents Are in the Military

Invitations to weddings involving members of the United States armed services follow the same general guidelines used for civilian weddings. The format and the wording are the same. The only difference is in the use of titles. While civilians use social titles such as "Mr.," "Mrs.," and the professional title of "Doctor" for medical doctors, military personnel use their military titles, which many times include their rank and branch of service. Military titles should not be abbreviated.

For more information on military weddings see page 76.

Bride's Mother Uses Her Maiden Name

Your mother's name should appear on the first line of the invitation and your father's name, preceded by "and" on the second. Either the titles of "Ms." and "Mr." or no titles are used in this format.

Mary Ellen Chance
and Andrew Jay Forrester
request the honour of your presence
at the marriage of their daughter
etc.

Father Does Not Wish to Use Middle Name

Formal wedding invitations require the use of full names, and never initials. If your father insists on not using his middle name, it's best to simply omit it entirely.

Father's Middle Name Is Just an Initial

As long as the initial is truly his full middle name, it may be used.

Divorced Parents

Some of the most difficult situations in wording wedding invitations occur when the parents of the bride are divorced. There are simple and straightforward rules to handle these situations but sometimes emotions take control of circumstances and render these rules inadequate. You may find yourself unable to follow the prescribed rules of etiquette to a tee for fear of offending a family member or creating additional, unnecessary tensions. If you find yourself in this situation, you may choose to go a different route and find wording that is both appropriate and innocuous. Etiquette is intended as a guide to good taste and to facilitate good relationships and the comfort of everyone. Therefore, in such an instance it is entirely appropriate for you to stray from the accepted rules.

The proper way to word an invitation when the bride's parents are divorced is to list the names of the bride's parents at the top of the invitation. Her mother's name is on the first line and her father's name is on the line beneath it. The lines are not separated by "and." If "and" were to be included between the names of divorced parents, it would create an additional line and a competing center of attention. With the extra line your eye is drawn to both the top of the invitation and the center. It should be drawn directly to the center where the names of the bride and groom appear.

Parents Are Divorced and Mother Has Not Remarried

In instances where the bride's mother had taken her former husband's name during marriage and has not remarried, she uses either "Mrs." or "Ms." followed by her first name, maiden name, and married name. The old etiquette called for using just her maiden name and her last name, preceded by "Mrs." The change evolved over the years as it was increasingly felt that the old usage was too impersonal.

Parents Are Divorced and Mother Has Remarried

When the bride's mother is divorced from the bride's father and has remarried and taken a new name, she uses "Mrs." followed by her current husband's full name.

Divorced Mother, Remarried, but Using Maiden Name

Depending upon your and your mother's preference, her name may appear without a title or with "Ms." preceding it. When "Ms." is not used, all other titles should be omitted so that the invitation retains a uniform appearance.

Parents Are Divorced and Father Has Remarried

Traditionally, you are "given away" by your parents. Therefore, it is generally only the names of your natural parents that properly appear on your wedding invitations. However, you may choose to set your own course for handling this matter by having your mother's name with a social title, either "Mrs." or "Ms.," appear on the first line. Your father and his new bride can be represented on the second line with "Mr. and Mrs." followed by your father's name. Your father's new wife's first name should not appear.

Including Stepparents on Invitations

It is your choice to follow or not follow the strict rules of etiquette. If you are more interested in including your extended family on your invitation than adhering to tradition, by all means do so.

This type of wording is often handled by listing the mother and her new husband's name on the first line and presented as "Mr. and Mrs." The father and his new wife's names appear on the second line as "Mr. and Mrs." The word "and" is typically not used to join the two lines but if relations between the couples are good and you feel it's appropriate, you may include it.

Inclusion of Father's Wife (not the Bride's Mother) on an Invitation

Etiquette should never be adhered to at the cost of damaging a relationship. Its purpose is to build relationships, not to harm them. There are ways to handle any situation that will accommodate everybody involved.

Many brides choose to have their mother's name on the first line followed by a second line reading "Mr. and Mrs." followed by the father's name. Again, the word "and" is not used to join the two lines.

Parents Are Divorced and Father Is Paying for the Wedding

Wedding invitations are worded the way they are to reflect the tradition of the bride's family graciously giving away the bride while inviting family and friends to join them for this happy occasion. As with the ceremony itself, the center of attention is the bride and groom. (That's why their names are spread out in the center of the invitation.) Therefore, there is no place to indicate who is paying the bills. To do so would be to draw attention away from the bride and groom.

If, after this explanation, you still feel a need to let people know that your father is picking up the tab, you may do so on the reception cards. The reception cards serve as invitations to the reception. By listing your father as host of the reception, you will be indicating to your guests that he is paying for it. This way, you have properly worded wedding invitations and reception cards that convey to your guests the fact that your father is funding the wedding.

Instead of reading "Reception / immediately following the ceremony," your reception cards should read, "Mr. Andrew Jay Forrester / requests the pleasure of your company / at the marriage reception" followed by the date, time, and place.

Separated Parents

When the bride's parents are legally separated, they may issue their daughter's wedding invitations together. Their names appear on separate lines with the name of the bride's mother on the first line and the bride's father's name on the second line. The word "and" is not used to join their names. Because they are separated but not divorced, the bride's mother name should appear as it did when she was married. If she took her husband's name at marriage, it would appear as "Mrs." followed by her husband's name. If she is not comfortable with this, she may use her own full name preceded by "Mrs." or "Ms." Another option is to have her name appear without any title. This approach, however, requires the dropping of all other titles on the invitation in order to keep the rest of the invitation uniform.

Widowed Parents

When one of the bride's parents is deceased, her wedding invitations are issued by her surviving parent. Traditionally, his or her name appears alone on the host line. In most cases, stepparents' names are not used (see page 51 for exceptions to this rule).

A widow retains the use of her husband's name. If she has not remarried, she continues to be known as "Mrs." Andrew Jay Forrester. If she has remarried, she uses "Mrs." followed by her present husband's name. In this case, since the bride's surname is different from her mother's surname, the bride's full name appears on the fourth line of the invitation. The bride's name is not preceded by "Miss."

BRIDE'S MOTHER HAS NOT REMARRIED:

Mrs. Paul James Travis

BRIDE'S MOTHER HAS REMARRIED:

Mrs. Glenn Lincoln Sanderson
requests the pleasure of your company
at the marriage of her daughter
Christina Lee Travis

BRIDE'S FATHER:

Mr. Paul James Travis

The Use of "Senior" and "Junior"

A man who is a "junior" usually stops using "junior" upon his father's death. If he is married, his widowed mother uses "senior" to distinguish herself from her daughter-in-law. "Senior" should be spelled out using a lowercase "s". It may be abbreviated to "Sr." when used with an especially long name.

Name of Widowed Mother

A widow who has not remarried should use her deceased husband's name, preceded by "Mrs." (A divorced woman uses "Mrs." followed by her first, maiden, and married names.) If your mother would rather use her first name, she can use "Ms." as a title or her name may appear without any title. The appearance of her name without titles makes the invitation slightly less formal and requires that all other titles be left off the invitation as well. This is done to keep the wording of the invitation consistent.

Inclusion of Deceased Parent's Name

While wishing to include a deceased parent's name on a wedding invitation is a lovely sentiment, it is not proper to do so (except in Latin cultures). The essential purpose of a wedding invitation is to invite your guests to your wedding and to tell them where and when it is taking place. It lists the host or hosts of the event, what the event is (your wedding), and the date, time, and place. The only logical place to list your father's name is on the host line. This, however, would indicate he is one of the hosts of your wedding and would be inappropriate given he is deceased.

Your father's name is, of course, mentioned in your newspaper announcement and may also be mentioned in the wedding program and during a prayer said during the service. Your wedding is a joyous occasion. Reminding your guests of your father's death by adding "and the late Mr. Andrew Jay Forrester" introduces an element of sadness to an otherwise joyous occasion.

The Hispanic tradition, on the other hand, does include the name of a deceased parent. If the deceased parent is the bride's father, her mother's name appears alone on the first line and her father's name, followed by a small cross if Christian or a Star of David if Jewish, appears on line two. One note of caution: Your guests may not be familiar with this custom and may not understand the meaning of it. If you are planning to have a program at your ceremony, this would be an ideal place to explain the symbols and their meaning.

Mrs. John Carlos Aponte

Mr. John Carlos Aponte †

request the honour of your presence

at the marriage of their daughter

etc.

Invitations Issued by the Couple

Although it is considered most proper for the parents of the bride to issue their daughter's wedding invitations, there may be times when the couple chooses to issue the invitations themselves. This most commonly occurs when the bride's parents are deceased, when the couple is older, the ceremony is a same-sex union, or when one of the couple is marrying for the second time.

If you issue your wedding invitations yourselves, your guests will probably assume that you and your fiancé are paying for the wedding. You may also have your parents issue the invitations to the ceremony while you and your fiancé issue the invitations to the reception.

There are two proper formats for self-invitations. The more formal of the two contains no host line. The less formal format lists both the bride and groom as hosts.

The honour of your presence

is requested at the marriage of

Miss Jennifer Marie Forrester

to

Mr. Nicholas Jude Strickland

etc.

OR:

Miss Jennifer Marie Forrester

and

Mr. Nicholas Jude Strickland

request the honour of your presence

etc.

Invitations Issued by the Groom's Parents

On rare occasions, perhaps when the bride's parents are deceased or when they live in a foreign country, the groom's parents may issue the wedding invitations. The format is a little different from the standard format. The parents' relationship to the groom is mentioned on the fifth line of the invitation instead of on the third line. This way, the invitations can still be read as the bride being married to the groom. Both the bride and the groom use their full names, preceded by their titles.

Mr. and Mrs. John Peter Strickland

request the honour of your presence

at the marriage of

Miss Jennifer Marie Forrester

to their son

Mr. Nicholas Jude Strickland

etc.

Invitations Issued by Other Relatives

Any member of the bride's family may host her wedding and issue the invitations when the bride's parents are deceased. The bride's relationship to her relatives issuing the invitation is designated on the third line of the invitation where the word "daughter" normally appears. The bride's full name minus her title appears on the following line.

Mr. and Mrs. David Allen Forrester

request the honour of your presence

at the marriage of their granddaughter

Jennifer Marie Forrester

etc.

Invitations Issued by Friends of the Bride

Friends of the bride may issue wedding invitations when the bride's parents are deceased and she has no close relatives. When friends issue the invitations, no relationship is shown on the third line and the bride's full name, preceded by "Miss," appears on the following line.

Mr. and Mrs. Charles Douglas Goldman

request the honour of your presence

at the marriage of

Miss Jennifer Marie Forrester

etc.

Request Line

The request line invites your guests to your ceremony. The wording varies according to where the event is being held. The correct wording for a wedding held in a church, temple, synagogue, or any house of worship is "request the honour of your presence." The word "honour" (also properly spelled as "honor") is used to show deference to God whenever a wedding is held in a house of worship. For weddings held in any location other than a house of worship, "request the pleasure of your company" is used.

Bride's Name

Traditionally, a young bride uses only her given name and middle name on an invitation issued by her parents. She uses neither an honorific nor surname since it is assumed that she had never married and has the same surname as her parents. Today's bride often chooses to use her given name, middle name, and surname because she has established herself independently from her parents and prefers to use her full name. In both cases, the name appears without the honorific "Miss."

When the bride's surname is different from the surname of whoever issues the invitations, she uses her given name, middle name, and surname.

A divorced woman uses her present name. That could be given name, maiden name, and married surname if she has continued to use her married surname, or it could be her given name, middle name, and maiden name if she has reverted to using them. She does not use an honorific.

A woman who had a previous marriage annulled may use "Miss," but the use of "Miss" has declined so much among women that most such brides simply use their name without an honorific.

A widow uses her present name. Traditionally, that name would be "Mrs. (husband's full name)," and that use of "Mrs." is still an option, but she can also choose to use her given name, maiden name, and married surname without an honorific.

Bride Is a Doctor

If the bride is a medical doctor, her title may appear on the invitation. The title precedes the bride's name and no advanced degrees appear after it. "Doctor" should be spelled out, not abbreviated. Those holding a PhD do not properly use their academic title.

Bride Is in the Military

If the bride is in the military, her rank should be included on the invitation. Titles should never be abbreviated. The branch of service should be listed on the line below the bride's name.

Lieutenant Colonel and Mrs. William Matthew Hoag

request the honour of your presence

at the marriage of their daughter

Captain Marissa Lynne Hoag

United States Air Force

to

Mr. Derek Hunter Healy

etc.

The Names of the Bride and Groom

If you look closely at a wedding invitation, you will notice that all the proper names (the bride, groom, bride's parents, and church) are highlighted since these are the most important lines. The names of the bride and groom stand out even more because of the very short line ("to" or "and") that separates them.

Bride Is a Lawyer

If the bride is an attorney her profession is not noted on the invitation. Lawyers once used "esquire" after their name to designate their profession on social invitations. In England, the title means "gentleman" and is used to honor a man when addressing him and therefore would not be an appropriate reference for a woman under any circumstance.

Joining Word

The joining word is the word that joins the names of the couple. The preposition "to" is used on invitations to the wedding ceremony as the bride is traditionally married to the groom. The conjunction "and" is used on invitations to the reception since the reception is given in honor of the couple. "And" is also used on Jewish wedding invitations, for Nuptial Masses, and on invitations issued by the couple.

Groom's Name

Traditionally, the groom always uses his full name, preceded by his title. If, however, the parents' names are not preceded by titles, the couple may choose to drop it from the groom's name for the sake of consistency.

There are no abbreviations, except for "Mr." All other titles, such as "Doctor" and "The Reverend" should be written out, although "Doctor" may be abbreviated when used with a long name. If "Doctor" is used more than once on an invitation, its use should be consistent. If it is necessary to abbreviate it with one of the names, it should be abbreviated with all names.

Initials are never properly used on formal wedding invitations. Men who dislike their middle names and use their middle initial instead should be discouraged from doing so. If your fiancé declines to use his middle name, it is better to omit his middle name entirely than to use just his initial.

Groom Is a Junior

Properly, "junior" is written out. Abbreviating "junior" to "Jr." is less formal but still acceptable. When written out, a lowercase "j" is used. When abbreviated, the "J" is capitalized. The abbreviation is commonly used when the groom has an exceptionally long name. A comma always precedes "junior" or "Jr."

Groom Is a Junior but His Father Is Deceased

"Junior" is used to distinguish a son from his father when they share a name. A man who is a "junior" usually stops using "junior" upon his father's death. Of course, if either the son or his father was a well-known public or private figure, the son would continue to use "junior" to avoid any confusion.

The Use of "Junior" and "II"

Although it may seem as though "junior" and the "II" can be used interchangeably, they are actually different designations. "Junior" is used by a man whose father has the same name that he has, whereas the "II" is used by a man who has the same name as an older relative other than the father.

The "III" is used by the namesake of a man using "junior" or "II." When used on an invitation, a comma usually precedes the "II" or "III." Some men prefer to omit the comma. Either way is correct.

Groom Is a Doctor

Medical doctors properly use their professional titles on wedding invitations, whereas PhDs do not. The word "Doctor" should be spelled out unless your fiancé's name is exceptionally long.

Medical degrees, such as MD or DDS, are never mentioned. They are professional designations that do not belong on a social invitation. Their use should be reserved for business cards and professional letterheads.

Groom Is in the Military

Your fiancé's rank should appear before his name. Military titles should never be abbreviated. Your fiancé's branch of service should appear on the line below his name.

Mr. and Mrs. Frederick Michael Barber

request the honour of your presence

at the marriage of their daughter

Catherine Louise

to

Lieutenant John Patrick Wyman

United States Army

etc.

Groom Is a Lawyer

If the groom is an attorney his profession is not noted on the invitation. While some lawyers use "esquire" to designate their status as attorneys, "esquire" is not recognized as a proper title in the United States. In England, the title means "gentleman" and is used to honor a man when addressing him. For a man to bestow that designation upon himself is considered presumptuous and in poor taste.

Use of Nicknames

Nicknames are never properly used on traditional wedding invitations. The names on the bride's and groom's birth certificates should be used.

Date Line

The day of the week and the date are written out in full. Abbreviations are not used. For some styles of invitations, the use of numerals rather than spelled-out numbers is more appropriate. The day of the week is first, followed by the date of the month and the month itself. The day of the week may be preceded by "on." The use of "on," however, is unnecessary and may make the line too long.

You may include the time of day, as in, "Saturday evening." That is not usually necessary, however, as most people are able to determine whether your invitation is for the morning or evening without specifically being told. For example, an invitation reading "at six o'clock" is obviously meant for six o'clock in the evening. If that invitation were meant for six o'clock in the morning, it would then be necessary to include "Saturday morning" since that would be unusual.

Invitations for weddings held at eight, nine, or ten o'clock should designate morning or evening since weddings are held at those times during both mornings and evenings. Many Roman Catholic weddings, for example, are held at those times in the mornings since most Nuptial Masses are held before noon, while some Jewish weddings are held at those times on Saturday evenings so the guests and participants can wait until after sundown to travel on the Sabbath.

The time of day can be noted on the Time Line instead.

Year Line

Since wedding invitations are sent four to six weeks before the wedding, it is not necessary to include the year. Your guests will assume that the invitation is for the next August twenty-third and not for some other August twenty-third in the distant future.

Although it is not necessary to include the year on your invitation, it is not improper to do so. Your invitations will, undoubtedly, be saved by you or your family and friends as a remembrance and may even be passed down to your children, grandchildren, and great-grandchildren. Including the year on your invitation will help your descendants remember your wedding day.

There are a couple of cautions, though, about including the year. First, many lettering styles, especially some of the script lettering styles, look better with fewer lines of copy. Additional lines might make your invitation look too cluttered.

Second, the year line is a long, heavy line that follows two other heavy lines (the groom's name and the date). This creates a lot of weight in that part of the invitation, which can draw your eye there instead of to the names of the bride and groom, where it should be drawn.

Wedding announcements, on the other hand, are sent after the wedding has taken place. Therefore, it is necessary to include the year or it could be assumed that your wedding took place on any August twenty-third in the past.

Capitalization in the Year Line

It is quite common for people to question whether or not the "T" in "two thousand" should be uppercase or lowercase in the year line. Although both ways are proper and many older invitations use all lowercase letters on the year line, almost all invitations nowadays capitalize the first letter. This usage is so common that not to do it might make it look as though your stationer forgot to capitalize the first letter. Furthermore, your invitations will look more polished if the first letter of the year is capitalized.

Time Line

An old superstition claims that being married on the half hour brings good fortune since the minute hand is ascending toward heaven, while being married on the hour leads to a bad marriage since, as with the minute hand, it is all downhill from there. Perhaps it is best to be married at noon when both hands are in the praying position.

No matter what the specific hour, the time of the wedding is presented on one line and all letters are lowercase. If your wedding is being held at six o'clock, the time line simply reads "at six o'clock." The time line for weddings held at six-thirty reads "at half after six o'clock."

The time line can be used to designate the time of day by using either "in the morning," "in the afternoon," or "in the evening." For most times it is not usually necessary, since a wedding held at six o'clock is obviously being held in the evening. Weddings held at eight, nine, or ten o'clock are another matter, since they could be held in either the morning or the evening. In those cases, a designation denoting the time of day is helpful. In any event, you may include the time of day, as was done in the past, if you find it aesthetically pleasing.

Weddings at Noon

Your invitations should simply read "at twelve o'clock." Unless otherwise noted, "twelve o'clock" means "noon."

If you feel strongly about indicating the time of day, you may use "at twelve o'clock in the afternoon."

Weddings at Forty-five Minutes After

The correct wording for 6:45 is "at three-quarters after six o'clock." Although correct, the wording may appear awkward to many people, so it might be a good idea to change the time of your wedding to six-thirty or seven o'clock.

Location

Wedding ceremonies are held at a variety of locations including churches, temples, synagogues, clubs, and even at home. The location line tells your guests the name of the location at which your wedding is being held. The full name of the facility is always given, so the location line for the wedding held at a church, for example, uses the full corporate name of the church. There should be no abbreviations. "Saint" is always spelled out. Likewise, a church commonly referred to as "Saint Matthew's Church" might actually be "Church of Saint Matthew" or "Saint Matthew's Roman Catholic Church." You should check with a clergyman or the church secretary to ascertain the correct name of the church.

Weddings at Home

While most wedding ceremonies are held in churches, hotels, and country clubs, many are held at home. The ceremony can be a religious one or a civil one. (Some religions, however, require that their wedding ceremonies be held in their place of worship.) The location is simply your parents' address. Since your wedding is taking place outside a house of worship, "request the pleasure of your company" is used.

Garden Weddings

It is always helpful to mention that the wedding will be a garden wedding to ensure that your guests wear appropriate footwear. A line reading "in the garden" appears above the address.

Wedding at a Friend's Home

If your wedding is being hosted at a friend's house, your friend's name and address are shown at the end of the invitation.

· POINTS OF STYLE ·

The Use of Corner Lines

Although reception cards are not necessary when a wedding and reception are being held at the same place, they may be used to convey your reply information. The reception cards read as they would if your reception were being held elsewhere. The name of the facility and its address, however, may be omitted since they are already given on the invitations.

Outdoor Weddings

One of the risks involved in having an outdoor wedding is that you are at the mercy of the elements. You may enclose a small "rain card" with your invitations that reads, "In case of inclement weather / the wedding will be held at / Sleepy Hollow Country Club / Scarborough." Of course, all of your guests will have different definitions of inclement weather. A cloudy wedding day may produce a very large number of phone calls. If you are planning an outdoor wedding, a tent would be much wiser investment than a bad-weather enclosed card.

Wedding at a Chapel at a Church

The name of the chapel may be given on the line directly above the name of the church. Your wording should begin with the specifics of the location (i.e. chapel or room) and move to the more general (i.e. church or hall) from there.

Wedding and Reception Held at the Same Place

When a wedding ceremony and reception are held in the same location, a line reading either "and afterwards at the reception" or "and afterward at the reception" is included on the invitations. This line appears at the end of the body of the invitation, beneath the city and state.

Mr. and Mrs. Andrew Jay Forrester

request the pleasure of your company

at the marriage of their daughter

Jennifer Marie

to

Nicholas Jude Strickland

Saturday, the twenty-third of August

at six o'clock

at the residence of

Mr. and Mrs. Michael Anthony LaPointe

217 Old Orchard Road

Bedford, New York

and afterwards at the reception

Street Address

The accepted rule on the use of the street address is that its inclusion is optional unless there is more than one facility with that name in that town, in which case it is mandatory. The street address is also used when the facility is not well known or when there are a number of out-of-town guests. Since giving the street address is an additional courtesy to your guests, it is almost always proper. The only time its use is not proper is when direction and map cards are used. Then the street address is redundant. Including the street address, however, adds an extra line to the invitation. Most invitations, especially those engraved in script lettering styles, look better with fewer lines of copy, so before you decide to include the address, consider the aesthetics.

City and State

The last line in the main body of the invitation shows the names of the city and state in which your wedding is being held. Both city and state are included, and are separated by a comma.

Two exceptions to this rule are New York City and Washington, D.C. For weddings held in New York, "New York City" or just "New York" are used since "New York, New York" seems redundant. The city and state line for weddings held in Washington, D.C., can read "City of Washington" or "Washington, District of Columbia."

RELIGIOUS AND CULTURAL CONSIDERATIONS

Roman Catholic Weddings

The Roman Catholic Church requires the posting of banns, the public announcement of a couple's intentions to marry. The banns must be announced from the pulpit or in the church bulletin three times before the wedding. The traditional posting of the banns was the forerunner of wedding announcements in the newspaper.

Catholics can be married in a simple wedding service or in a Nuptial Mass. A Nuptial Mass is a wedding ceremony performed as part of the Catholic Mass (or service). When the wedding ceremony will be a Nuptial Mass, the invitations should mention that a Nuptial Mass will be performed. Nuptial Masses are about an hour long. Placing the phrase "Nuptial Mass" on the wedding invitations alerts guests to the fact that the wedding will take a little longer than what they might be accustomed.

Nuptial Masses were once performed only at or before noon but are now performed in the afternoon as well. Unless special permission is granted by the bishop, Nuptial Masses may not be performed during Lent or Advent.

As suggested by the invitations, the bride and groom are joined together in holy matrimony. Therefore, "and" is used instead of "to."

Mr. and Mrs. Andrew Jay Forrester

request the honour of your presence

at the Nuptial Mass uniting their daughter

Jennifer Marie

and

Mr. Nicholas Jude Strickland

Saturday, the twenty-third of August

at nine o'clock in the morning

Saint Matthew's Roman Catholic Church

Scarborough, New York

Jewish Weddings

According to Jewish tradition, marriages are made in heaven. Men and women are brought together to marry one another by God Himself. Women are not married "to" men. Rather, men and women are joined together in marriage. Because of this tradition, the joining word on Jewish wedding invitations reads "and" instead of "to."

Jewish custom also celebrates the joining of the two families, so the names of the groom's parents always appear on the invitations. Their names most properly appear beneath the groom's name and a line reading "son of Mr. and Mrs. Solomon Lang" or on two lines that read "son of / Mr. and Mrs. Solomon Lang." Their names may also appear at the top of the invitations beneath the names of the bride's parents. This is done occasionally by parents of the bride who feel that they honor the groom's parents more by placing their names at the top of the invitation. When this is done, the request line reads "at the marriage of." The bride, in this case, uses her full name but no title. The groom's title is omitted as well to maintain uniformity.

· POINTS OF STYLE ·

Celebrating Marriage

Because the Jewish invitation reflects a celebration of marriage and participation of the guests, the traditional language of "request the honour of your presence" is often replaced with an invitation to "dance at" or to "share in the joy of."

Hebrew lettering is often used on Jewish wedding invitations. It may take the form of a quotation from the wedding blessing, blind-embossed across the top of the invitations, or the entire invitation text may be reproduced in Hebrew on a part of the invitation. When the invitation appears in both English and Hebrew, the Hebrew version appears on the right-inside page.

For reform couples, in lieu of full Hebrew text, many invitations will simply have their names written in Hebrew, next to the English version, or the date of the wedding in Hebrew.

Mr. and Mrs. David Green
request the honour of your presence
at the marriage of their daughter
Deborah
to
Mr. Steven Lang
son of
Mr. and Mrs. Solomon Lang
Sunday, the twenty-fourth of August
at six o'clock
Temple Beth-El
Scarsdale, New York

Orthodox Services

If your service includes a Hakhnassat Kallah (bride's reception), a Chatan's Tish (groom's reception), and a bedeken prior to the service at the same location, you may mention these events directly on the invitation. Alternatively, an insert similar to a reception card may also be used to inform and invite your guests.

Use of "at the marriage of their children"

While it is equally correct to use "at the marriage of their children" and "at the marriage of," many people feel that if a couple is old enough to get married, they are no longer children.

Mr. and Mrs. David Green

Mr. and Mrs. Solomon Lang

request the honour of your presence

at the marriage of

Deborah Ruth Green

and

Steven Matthew Lang

etc.

· POINTS OF STYLE ·

Wedding Programs

Programs are particularly helpful for guests at interfaith marriages or any time the guest list includes a number of people who may not be familiar with the rituals and traditions of the ceremony.

Mormon Weddings

Members of the Church of Jesus Christ of Latter-day Saints are married or "sealed" for "time and eternity" in temples open only to practicing Latter-day Saints. Weddings are generally small and intimate, attended by family and very close friends. The reception afterward is a much larger affair to which all friends and all members of the bride and groom's extended families are invited. Since more guests are invited to the reception than to the ceremony, the invitations are for the reception. Ceremony cards enclosed with the reception invitations are sent to those guests who are also invited to the temple ceremony.

Mr. and Mrs. Andrew Jay Forrester

request the pleasure of your company

at the marriage reception of their daughter

Jennifer Marie

and

Mr. Nicholas Jude Strickland

son of

Mr. and Mrs. John Peter Strickland

following their marriage

in the Salt Lake L.D.S. Temple

Saturday, the twenty-third of August

from seven until nine o'clock

La Caille at Quail Run

Salt Lake City, Utah

Invitations to Latter-day Saint wedding receptions differ from standard reception invitations in that they mention that the wedding ceremony was performed in the Latter-day Saint temple. Because Latter-day Saints place great emphasis on the importance of families, the groom's parents are honored by having their names mentioned on wedding invitations. Their names appear beneath the groom's name, preceded by "son of" on a separate line. Guests drop in and out of Latter-day Saint receptions. They arrive to congratulate the newlyweds and stay for a while to talk to friends and to renew acquaintances. Then they leave and go on their way. Consequently, the time line on the invitations mentions the time period during which the reception will be held.

Ceremony cards draw a distinction between weddings held in a Mormon temple and weddings held elsewhere. When weddings are held in a temple, it is so noted on the ceremony card.

Inclusion of a Photo with an Invitation

It is very common in the Latter-day Saints community to include photographs with, or even feature them on, the invitations. While old rules of etiquette would deem photos superfluous, it is certainly considered acceptable and, in some circles, expected, to include them.

Hispanic Weddings

Traditional invitations to Hispanic weddings are issued by both sets of parents. The names of the bride's parents are always listed first.

Hispanic invitations can be done in a number of different formats. They may be produced on one page, in English or Spanish, with the names of the bride's parents listed separately on the first two lines, "and" on the third line, and names of the groom's parents listed on the following two lines.

They may also be produced in both languages on the two inside pages of the invitations. The left-inside page may appear in Spanish while the right-inside page appears in English. When this format is used, the parents' names appear as described above.

Another frequently used format for Hispanic wedding invitations is an invitation where text appears on the two inside pages. The right-inside page is an invitation from the groom's parents and the left-inside page is an invitation from the bride's parents. Common copy, such as date, time, and place may be combined in the center of the invitation.

Customs may vary from one Latin American country to another. If you have any questions concerning the etiquette practiced in a particular country, it is best to call the protocol officer in their consulate for answers.

José Hernandez Caratini

Carmen Maria de Hernandez

y

Juan Martinez Garza

Consuela Elena de Martinez

tienen el honor de invitarle

al matrimonio de sus hijos

Linda

y

Roberto

el sabado diez de Julio

de mil novecientos noventa y siete

a las dos de la tarde

Santa Iglesia Catedral

San Juan de Puerto Rico

José Hernandez Caratini
Carmen Maria de Hernandez
request the honour of your presence
at the marriage of their daughter
Linda
to
Roberto Martinez

Juan Martinez Garza
Consuela Elena de Martinez
request the honour of your presence
at the marriage of
Linda Hernandez
to their son
Roberto

Saturday, the tenth of July
Two thousand ten
at two o'clock
Santa Iglesia Cathedral

San Juan, Puerto Rico

Indian Weddings

While Indian weddings may be conducted in the tradition of Hindu, Bengali, Kashmiri, Maharashtrian, Muslim, Punjabi, Gujarati, Arya Samaj, Telugu, Temil, or a combination of faiths, the event is far from a solemn and serious occasion. The wedding celebration is much more akin to a festival that lasts for several days and includes a great deal of color and music. The celebratory feel of the event is often reflected in the invitation.

A vibrant colored stock, very often a rich red or saffron, with an ornate border or motif reflecting the couple's Indian roots is traditional. Invitations to any related dance parties or celebrations sometimes share elements of the wedding invitation but it is not necessary. Wording of the invitation varies depending upon the type of service being held. Couples should consult with their designated officiant for the specific language to be used on the invitation.

Hindu Weddings

Traditional Hindu weddings are hosted by the parents of the bride, but if the bride's paternal grandparents are living, listing them as the hosts on the invitation is considered to be a gracious and joyous option.

Islamic Weddings

Traditional invitations to Islamic weddings, both Sunni and Shiite, follow the same formula of parents hosting a party for the couple.

The "nikah" is the first event and includes the ceremony and a reception. The parents of the bride host the "nikah" and are listed first on the invitation. Since the "nikah" includes the wedding, the wording "requests your presence at the marriage of their daughter" is the most appropriate. After the name of the groom, text notes "son of," and the names of the groom's parents. A reception follows the ceremony and so a reception card is often included.

A "valima" is the second event, usually the day after the "nikah" is hosted by the parents of the groom. It includes no religious ceremony, so the wording "request the pleasure of your company in honor of the marriage of their son" is most appropriate. The groom's name is listed first, then the bride's name, followed by "daughter of" and lists names of her parents.

Interfaith Marriages

Because interfaith marriages involve the blending of two sets of traditions and customs, there are no hard and fast rules for invitations. The most important thing is that the couple finds a way to reflect the nature of their union and service, while being respectful of each other's faiths.

Very often couples will use elements of the traditional wording and style of each faith on their invitation, thereby setting the tone and spirit of the union for their guests.

Bilingual Marriages

Bilingual invitations can be handled in any number of ways. Very often the invitation will appear in two columns, with the left column appearing in English and the right column in the second language appropriate for the family or guests of the bride and groom.

If space does not allow for a two-column format, a folded invitation can also be created with separate wording in the two native languages, facing one another.

Alternatively, a separate insert can be created in the second language and included with the reception card and other invitation elements.

MILITARY WEDDINGS

Invitations to weddings involving members of the armed services follow the same etiquette as civilian weddings, except that ranks, ratings, and branches of service must be considered when listing the names of active duty or retired service personnel.

The branch of service (Army, Navy, Air Force, Marine Corps, or Coast Guard) appears, unabbreviated and preceded by "United States," on a separate line beneath the name and rank, when the name of the armed services member appears on a line by itself. When an invitation is issued by an officer and his wife identified as "Mrs. (surname)," the service designation is omitted.

Civilian references traditionally suggest an Army, Air Force, and Marine officer with the rank of Captain or higher, and a Navy and Coast Guard officer with the rank of Commander or higher, lists his or her rank as an honorific (before the name) on a wedding invitation. These civilian references also recommend that a junior commissioned officer not use his or her rank as an honorific (before his or her name) on wedding invitations: These lower-ranking officers are directed to list their rank and service designation on a separate line below their name. However, within the armed services all officers use their ranks before their names on every type of invitation. So, ask the service member for his or her preference of which tradition to follow.

Civilian references traditionally also recommend a noncommissioned officer or enlisted person not use his or her rank or rating on a wedding invitation. These references suggest they list their full name on one line and their branch of service on a separate line: No reference is made to their rank or rating. However, within the armed services noncommissioned and enlisted personnel use their ranks or ratings before their name on every type of invitation. So, ask the service member for his or her preference of which tradition to follow.

When using ranks and ratings, be sure to use the correct form of the rank or rating. For example, officers hold the graded ranks of "General," "Lieutenant General," "Major General," and "Brigadier General," but on an invitation a simplified form of their full rank is used: all are listed as "General (name)." In contrast, a "Technical Sergeant" in the Air Force and a "Gunnery Sergeant" in the Marine Corps are addressed as "Sergeant (name)" and "Gunnery Sergeant (name)" respectively, reflecting different traditions in different branches of service.

Ranks and ratings are never abbreviated unless it is necessary due to space limitations.

The honorifics "Mr." or "Miss" are never used when listing any active-duty person.

Retired high-ranking officers have the option to continue to use their armed service rank as their honorific socially, and even professionally when working in the private sector after retirement. Retired junior officers, noncommissioned officers, and enlisted personnel do not normally continue to use their rank or rating.

No mention is made of the officer's retired status, unless the service designation is included.

Military Titles on Invitations

	BRIDE'S NAME	GROOM'S NAME
SENIOR OFFICER	Commander Christina Lee Travis United States Army	Major Andrew Jay Fannin United States Marine Corps
JUNIOR OFFICER	Christina Lee Travis Ensign, United States Army OR Ensign Christina Lee Travis United States Army	Andrew Jay Fannin First Lieutenant, United States Marine Corps OR First Lieutenant Andrew Jay Fannin United States Marine Corps
NONCOMMISSIONED OFFICER OR ENLISTED PERSON	Christina Lee Travis United States Army OR Christina Lee Travis Staff Sergeant, United States Army OR Staff Sergeant Christina Lee Travis United States Army	Andrew Jay Fannin United States Army OR Andrew Jay Fannin Master Sergeant, United States Army OR Master Sergeant Andrew Jay Fannin United States Army
	BRIDE'S PARENTS (MARRIED)*	BRIDE'S PARENTS (DIVORCED)**
FATHER IS A SENIOR OFFICER	Colonel and Mrs. Paul James Travis	Mrs. Laura Simpson Travis Colonel Paul James Travis United States Army
FATHER IS A JUNIOR OFFICER	Paul James Travis Lieutenant, United States Army and Mrs. Travis OR Lieutenant and Mrs. Paul James Travis	Mrs. Laura Simpson Travis Paul James Travis Lieutenant, United States Army OR Mrs. Laura Simpson Travis Lieutenant Paul James Travis United States Army
FATHER IS A NONCOMMISSIONED OFFICER OR ENLISTED MAN	Mr. and Mrs. Paul James Travis OR Sergeant Major and Mrs. Paul James Travis	Mrs. Laura Simpson Travis Paul James Travis United States Army OR Mrs. Paul James Travis Sergeant Major Paul James Travis
FATHER IS A RETIRED OFFICER	Colonel and Mrs. Paul James Travis	Mrs. Paul James Travis Colonel Paul James Travis United States Army, Retired

MOTHER IS A SENIOR OFFICER	Colonel Laura Simpson Travis United States Army and Mr. Paul James Travis	Colonel Laura Simpson Travis United States Army Mr. Paul James Travis
MOTHER IS A JUNIOR OFFICER	Laura Simpson Travis Lieutenant, United States Army and Mr. Paul James Travis OR Lieutenant Laura Simpson Travis United States Army and Mr. Paul James Travis	Laura Simpson Travis Lieutenant, United States Army Mr. Paul James Travis OR Lieutenant Laura Simpson Travis United States Army Mr. Paul James Travis
MOTHER IS A NONCOMMISSIONED OFFICER OR ENLISTED WOMAN	Laura Simpson Travis United States Army and Mr. Paul James Travis OR Laura Simpson Travis Chief Warrant Officer, United States Army and Mr. Paul James Travis OR Chief Warrant Officer Laura Simpson Travis United States Army and Mr. Paul James Travis	Laura Simpson Travis United States Army Mr. Paul James Travis OR Laura Simpson Travis Chief Warrant Officer, United States Army Mr. Paul James Travis OR Chief Warrant Officer Laura Simpson Travis United States Army Mr. Paul James Travis
MOTHER IS A RETIRED OFFICER	Colonel Laura Simpson Travis United States Army, Retired and Mr. Paul James Travis	Colonel Laura Simpson Travis United States Army, Retired Mr. Paul James Travis
BOTH PARENTS ARE OFFICERS	Colonel Laura Simpson Travis United States Army and Colonel Paul James Travis United States Army OR The Colonels Travis	Colonel Laura Simpson Travis United States Army Colonel Paul James Travis United States Army
BOTH PARENTS ARE RETIRED OFFICERS	Colonel Laura Simpson Travis United States Army, Retired and Colonel Paul James Travis United States Army, Retired	Colonel Laura Simpson Travis United States Army, Retired Colonel Paul James Travis United States Army, Retired

*The use of "and" before the second name indicates the hosts are married.**The absence of an "and" before the second name indicates the hosts are no longer married. In the examples above, the mother of the bride is shown to still be using her married name. See page 50 for other forms for a divorced mother of the bride.

REAFFIRMATIONS AND COMMITMENT CEREMONIES

Reaffirmation of Wedding Vows

A number of couples choose to celebrate their anniversaries by having a ceremony to renew their wedding vows. Other couples, married in a civil ceremony for one reason or another, choose to reaffirm their vows under religious auspices. As with any other invitation, invitations to reaffirmation ceremonies should reflect the level of formality of the occasion.

Mr. and Mrs. Nicholas Jude Strickland

request the honour of your presence

at a ceremony to celebrate

the reaffirmation of their wedding vows

Saturday, the twenty-third of August

at six o'clock

Church of Christ

Bedford, New York

and at a reception afterward

Sleepy Hollow Country Club

Scarborough

Special Circumstances

On occasion when a parent or loved one is bedridden, a couple will choose to have a bedside ceremony so that the ailing individual can be included. If a couple later chooses to have a traditional church ceremony, they may issue invitations in their parent's or parents' name or their own. The invitation should read as a reaffirmation of their wedding vows. If, however, the couple was married in a civil ceremony and now wishes to get married in a religious ceremony, the invitations would state that the ceremony was being performed to solemnize the marriage. (To solemnize means to make right before God.)

Mrs. Andrew Jay Forrester

requests the honour of your presence

at the religious ceremony to solemnize

the marriage of her daughter

Jennifer Marie

and

Mr. Nicholas Jude Strickland

etc.

Commitment Ceremonies

Couples planning their commitment ceremonies consider many of the same traditions as traditional brides and grooms do. Typically hosted by the couple or one or both sets of parents, the ceremony can be as formal or informal as the couple wishes. Some couples choose to have an officiant at their service while others prefer to have their own words, as well as those of friends and family, serve as the public proclamation of their commitment.

Invitation wording and styles can be just as unique as the ceremony. As with a traditional invitation, the most important thing is that it informs your guests of the date, time, location, and nature of the event. Other than that, each couple is free to choose the design, format, and elements that work for them.

BETHANY AND ELIZABETH

Mr. and Mrs. Thomas Alber
request the honour of your presence
at the commitment ceremony of their daughter

BETHANY LYNN ALBER

to

ELIZABETH HARRISON WILKINS

February 26, 2012, at two o'clock in the afternoon

Arlington Church   Boston, Massachusetts

Samples of invitations to
commitment ceremonies

TOGETHER WITH THEIR FAMILIES

TOM KLEIN AND JAKE CLAIBORNE

INVITE YOU TO SHARE IN THE JOYOUS BEGINNING
OF THEIR NEW LIFE TOGETHER

THE CELEBRATION OF THEIR COMMITMENT AND LOVE
WILL BE HELD ON
SATURDAY, THE FIFTH OF JUNE
TWO THOUSAND ELEVEN
AT SIX O'CLOCK IN THE EVENING
TOM NEVERS BEACH
NANTUCKET, MASSACHUSETTS

INVITATION ENCLOSURES

Reception Cards

Reception cards are used whenever the wedding ceremony and reception are held in different places. Because they are at different locations, they are considered separate events, each requiring its own invitation. Reception cards are not necessary when the ceremony and the reception are held at the same place.

An accompanying reply card allows your guests to notify you if they will or will not be able to attend the wedding and reception.

Composing a Reception Card

The first line on the reception card indicates the occasion. It reads "Breakfast" when occurring before one o'clock (regardless of the menu) and "Reception" when held at one o'clock or later.

The next line indicates the time and usually reads "immediately following the ceremony." This phrase should not be taken literally as it simply means that the reception will start in, more or less, the amount of time it takes to get from the ceremony to the reception. If the reception is scheduled to start two or more hours after the ceremony ends, the phrase "immediately following the ceremony" should be replaced with the appropriate time. The line may then read "at eight o'clock."

The name of the facility at which the reception will take place is given on the third line. The address is usually shown on the fourth line, although it is omitted whenever the facility is very well known or when directions and map cards are used.

The city and state follow on the next line if they are not the same as those shown on the invitation. If the city and state do not appear on the reception card, it is assumed that the reception is in the same town as the wedding. Likewise, if the city is different but the state is the same, you need only mention the city. These are options. You may, however, under any circumstances use both city and state.

Responses to Reception Cards

Historically, all social invitations were responded to through a handwritten note. However, over time this particular point of etiquette seems to have faded from the public consciousness and led to the development of reply cards. Most wedding invitation ensembles now include a reply card that serves as a response device for both the wedding and reception.

When reply cards are not being sent, a reply is requested in the lower left-hand corner of the reception card. Corner lines appear in a smaller size than the body of the reception card.

The top line asks your guests to reply by stating either "The favour of a reply is requested," "R.s.v.p.," or "R.S.V.P." All three are considered proper. However, in some regions, such as the southern United States, "The favour of a reply is requested" is preferred while "R.s.v.p." is frowned upon.

The address to which the replies are to be sent is shown on the following two lines. The address shown is the address of the person whose name first appears on the wedding invitation. So if the invitation was issued by your parents, the lines would contain your parents' address. If you would like to have the replies sent to you, you must put your name, preceded by your title, on the lines beneath the reply request.

Whether you use your address or your parents' address, you should always include an address on your reception cards to reply to even when the same address appears on the invitation's outside envelope (except when also sending reply cards). People tend to discard envelopes, especially when there is an additional inside envelope. If some of your guests throw out their envelopes and there is no address inside, they may not be able to reply. This could result in your having to make some unnecessary phone calls.

Reception

immediately following the ceremony

Sleepy Hollow Country Club

Scarborough, New York

The favour of a reply is requested
2830 Meadowbrook Drive
Bedford, New York 10506

• POINTS OF STYLE •

Favor versus Favour

The word "favor" can be correctly spelled as either "favor" or "favour." Like "honor" and honour," it is a matter of personal preference, although the vast majority of brides prefer the English spelling, "favour." If you use the English spelling of "honour," use the English spelling of "favour" also, for consistency.

Sit-down Dinners

In most cases, no special designation is needed to alert your guests to the fact that a dinner will be served at your reception. Many brides, however, worry that their guests might not know that a meal will be served and will make other plans for dinner. You may alert your guests about the dinner by including "Dinner Reception" on the top line of your reception cards.

Dancing

While some brides use "Dinner and Dancing" on the first line of their reception cards, it is usually not necessary to do so. If there is a band and a dance floor, people will dance.

Including or Excluding Children

The names of the family members that you are inviting are written on the inside envelope. If children are not invited to your wedding, their names are simply left off the inside envelope. Thus, when "Mr. and Mrs. Sterling" is written on the inside envelope, it means only that Mr. and Mrs. Sterling are invited, not their children. If their children were invited, the inside envelope would read:

Mr. and Mrs. Sterling

Kathryn, Robby, and John

Of course most people are not familiar with this point of etiquette and a corner line reading "No children, please" seems a bit cruel, so what else can you do? The best solution is to talk to your family members and friends with children and let them know that, although you would really love to invite their children, expenses (or whatever) prevent you from doing so. A possible compromise might be to invite children to the ceremony but not to the reception. This, too, is best handled by talking it over with those involved.

Formal Receptions

The time of day actually dictates the formality of dress for the wedding and reception. (After six o'clock is considered formal.) Although some people are familiar with this point of etiquette, most are not. Therefore, you may wish to include "Black tie" on your reception cards to ensure that all your guests know how to dress.

When using "Black tie," the "B" is uppercase and the "t" is lowercase. "Black tie" generally appears in the lower right-hand corner of the reception card. It does not appear on the invitation to the ceremony since it is the reception, not the ceremony, that is formal. When no reception card is used, "Black tie" appears in the lower right-hand corner of the invitation. If you do not like corner lines on invitations, you may include a reception card to indicate the type of dress.

White-Tie Attire

White-tie events are even more formal than black-tie events. They require men to wear white tie, wing collar, and tailcoat. Women wear evening gowns.

"Black tie optional"

While "Black tie optional" is sometimes used, it is not correct and may cause confusion since it literally means that you may dress any way you please, with a tuxedo being one of the acceptable choices. If you want to be assured that all your guests wear formal attire, you'll want to drop the "optional" from your wording.

Reception at Parents' Home

If your parents are hosting your wedding and their names are on the first line of the wedding invitations, the location lines on the reception card shows their home address. Your guests will know that it is their address because no other names are mentioned. When reply cards are not sent, the corner line on the reception card reads "The favour of a reply is requested," "R.s.v.p," or "R.S.V.P." Your parents' address is not shown beneath the reply request since it has already been given in the body of the reception card.

Reception at the Home of a Friend

When a reception is held at the home of a friend, your friend's name and address are given on the location lines. A line reading "at the residence of" precedes his or her name and address.

Reception

immediately following the ceremony

at the residence of

Mr. and Mrs. Michael Anthony LaPointe

211 Old Orchard Road

Bedford, New York

Reception on a Yacht

The wording for a reception to be held on a yacht is similar to the wording on a standard reception card. The location line reads "aboard the *Mirabell*" or whatever the name of the yacht is. The line beneath it shows the name of the yacht club or marina out of which it will sail.

In order to ensure that your guests do not miss the boat, you may add two lines to the lower right-hand corner of your reception cards that read "The *Mirabell* sails promptly at eight o'clock."

Wedding and Reception at Separate Locations

Weddings and receptions held at separate locations are considered separate events and require separate invitations. Reception cards serve as invitations to the reception and are used whenever the wedding and the reception are

• POINTS OF STYLE •
Wedding Gift and Registries

It is in very poor taste to include a card announcing the store at which you are registered. That is too much like asking for a gift. The best way to let people know is by word of mouth. If this is not practical, the save-the-date would be the least offensive place to include it. With the evolution of the web, many couples now have wedding home pages. The URL for the pages is often included on their save-the-date card. Registry information is often included on the website.

While an occasional bride and groom establish a money tree and ask their guests to contribute toward it, in some circles it is still considered incorrect and in very poor taste to ask your guests for money. First of all, it is presumptuous on your part to expect a gift from everybody to whom invitations are sent. Second, a number of your guests will probably want to give you a special gift to be remembered by. Asking for money directly is much too mercenary. (Of course, there is no reason why your parents, when asked, could not suggest a check.)

held in different locations. In the case of a formal wedding, the reception information should not appear on the wedding invitation itself.

If you are doing a less formal wedding invitation and wanted to combine the wedding and the reception information on one invitation, you could add a couple of lines to the invitation beneath the city and state that read "and afterward at the reception / Sleepy Hollow Country Club," "and afterward at the reception / Sleepy Hollow Country Club / Scarborough," or "Reception to follow / Sleepy Hollow Country Club / Scarborough."

Responding to a Reception Card

Social invitations should be responded to in writing. This includes the completion and return of an enclosed reply card. The use of a telephone, fax, or email for responses is reserved for business and informal social occasions.

Reply Cards

In the past, a wedding invitation was properly responded to through a handwritten note. Over time and owing to many factors, including a lack of understanding of social etiquette and increased demands on individual time, this tradition has fallen by the wayside and reply cards have become a standard element in current wedding invitation sets. (For more on how to prepare a handwritten response, see page 92.)

Reply cards can be produced in a number of different formats. All formats, however, share similar features. Spaces are always provided for the guests' names and for their responses. A request for a response is always included as well, usually before a specific date. The reply request may be made in either the first two lines of the reply card or in the lower left-hand corner. Some brides choose not to include a date in their reply request as they feel it might insult guests who know very well when to reply. The name and address of whoever will receive the replies appears on the face of the reply envelopes.

Alternative Formats for Reply Cards

Some couples prefer to receive handwritten responses to their invitations. One way to ensure handwritten responses are received is to send reply cards that are blank except for the words "The favour of a reply is requested" appear across the top or bottom of the card. A second possibility is to take a small fold-over note, turn it on its side so the fold is on the left-hand side, and engrave. This side-fold note becomes a miniature version of the letter sheet that is properly used for handwritten responses. It also seems to be a little more elegant than a card.

Selective Use of Reply Cards

If you are afraid of offending some of your guests by sending them reply cards, you may send reply cards just to those who you feel would need them. This, of course, requires two sets of reception cards; one with the reply request in the lower left-hand corner for those guests not receiving reply cards and another without the reply request for those guests who are receiving reply cards.

Omitting the "M" on a Reply Card

If the couple-to-be are both doctors and perhaps their parents are as well, it is likely that many of their guests will also be doctors. Given that, you may wish

· POINTS OF STYLE ·

Filling in Reply Cards

Reply cards are easier to use than they appear to be. A space, usually following an "M," is provided for your titles and names. (The "M" is provided to help you get started with your title, assuming your title begins with an "M." If it does not, you may draw a slash through the "M" and write out "Doctor" or whatever your title may be.) The next line allows you to tell your hosts whether or not you will be attending. If you are, the space is left blank. If you are unable to attend, you write in "not." You then place the card inside its envelope and mail it.

What names are used on reply cards?
Your full social names with titles are used. If you are married, your names read "Mr. and Mrs." followed by your husband's first, middle, and last names.

I received a blank card with just "The favour of a reply is requested" on it. What should I do?
Blank reply cards are sent when a bride would like a formal response but is afraid that if she does not send reply cards, she will not get many responses. Since the bride provided you the card and the opportunity to write a formal response, you should do so (see page 92 for more information).

to omit the "M" on the reply cards. This leaves your reply cards with a blank name line and allows your guests to write in their appropriate titles.

Meal Selection and Number of Guests

While once considered inappropriate, it is now not uncommon for meal selections to be included on the reply card. Just be mindful that the reply card is an appropriate size to accommodate the inclusion of additional information requests. A larger size may be necessary to keep the card looking neat and elegant.

Some couples also include a line requesting "number of guests" on their reply cards.

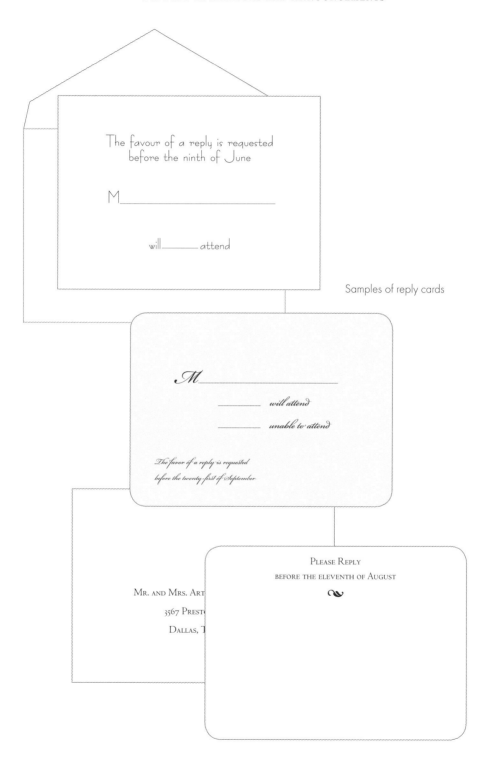

The favour of a reply is requested
before the ninth of June

M_____

will_____attend

Samples of reply cards

M_____

_____ *will attend*

_____ *unable to attend*

The favor of a reply is requested
before the twenty-first of September

PLEASE REPLY
BEFORE THE ELEVENTH OF AUGUST

Mr. and Mrs. Art

3567 Prest

Dallas, T

• POINTS OF STYLE •

Formal Handwritten Responses

Although most wedding invitations are sent with reply cards, many are sent with a reply request on the reception card instead. These invitations require a handwritten response. Formal responses are handwritten on ecru letter sheets. These sheets were traditionally blank but may now have a tasteful monogram blind-embossed on the top.

Responses follow the format of the invitations. Since wedding invitations are issued in the third person, responses are written in the third person as well. The guests' full social names and titles are used while only the hosts' titles and surnames are written. On the envelopes, however, the hosts' full names are used with their titles. Acceptances repeat the date and time while regrets repeat just the date. There is no need to mention the reason for not attending.

ACCEPTANCE:

Mr. and Mrs. Edward Allen Singer
accept with pleasure
the kind invitation of
Mr. and Mrs. Forrester
for Saturday, the twenty-third of August
at six o'clock

REGRET:

Mr. and Mrs. Edward Allen Singer
regret that they are unable to accept
the kind invitation of
Mr. and Mrs. Forrester
for Saturday, the twenty-third of August

IN WHAT COLOR INK SHOULD RESPONSES BE WRITTEN?

Formal responses may be written in blue or black ink. Most people, however, prefer black ink since it usually matches the invitations.

HOW IS THE RESPONSE WRITTEN WHEN CHILDREN ARE INVITED?

The names used in your response should be the same as those written on the inside envelope you received. If your children are invited, their names will be listed on the face of the inside envelope, beneath yours. When writing your response, repeat the names as they are written on the inside envelope.

Mr. and Mrs. Edward Allen Singer

Esta, Janice, and Barbara

accept with pleasure

etc.

MY HUSBAND AND I WERE BOTH INVITED TO MY COUSIN'S WEDDING. I WILL BE ABLE TO GO BUT MY HUSBAND WILL BE OUT OF TOWN. HOW SHOULD MY RESPONSE READ?

Your response begins with a formal acceptance on your part. Your husband's regret is added at the end.

Mrs. Edward Allen Singer

accepts with pleasure

the kind invitation of

Mr. and Mrs. Forrester

for Saturday, the twenty-third of August

at six o'clock

Mr. Edward Allen Singer

regrets that he is unable to attend

Although having your guests fill in a space asking how many of them will be attending would definitely help you in obtaining an accurate count for the caterer, there is one very serious drawback. By doing so, you encourage your guests to bring along more people than you otherwise would have invited. An invitation addressed to "Mr. and Mrs. Smith" with a reception card asking them how many people are coming might lead them to think that not only are they invited but also their kids and, perhaps, their Aunt Sally who, as it happens, will be in town that week. Giving your guests an opportunity like that can be asking for trouble.

Reply-by Dates

Most couples ask that their replies be received two weeks before their wedding date. Caterers, restaurants, clubs, and other locations typically look for a final count five days before the event. When choosing your venue, be sure to ask the manager about the timeframe for a specific count.

Reply Envelopes

Reply envelopes must always be included when a reply card is provided. The address of the issuer of the wedding invitation, not the bride or groom, should appear on the face of the envelope. While the inclusion of return postage is a matter of choice, most people include it as a common courtesy to their guests.

Postage

There are two schools of thought when it comes to pre-stamping the reply envelope. Some people feel quite strongly that guests should feel honored to be invited to the wedding and more than willing to provide a stamp for their response. Others believe that providing a stamp is a matter of common courtesy and, given that guests may incur expenses related to travel and lodging around the wedding, it is a small price to pay to make a guest feel welcome.

The best advice is to do what feels right to you. Your guests will no doubt respond no matter which course you choose.

At-home Cards

Family and friends can be made aware of your new address when at-home cards are included with your invitations and announcements. At-home cards are small enclosure cards whose card stock, lettering style, and ink color match the invitations with which they are sent. They alert people of the address at which you will be residing and the date after which you will be there (most couples use the date on which they return from their honeymoon). Many couples now include their phone numbers and email addresses on their at-home cards.

The wording for at-home cards sent with announcements is different from the wording for at-home cards sent with the invitations. At-home cards sent with announcements show your names together as "Mr. and Mrs." since you are already married when they are sent. When sent with invitations your names are not used since you are not yet married and cannot use "Mr. and Mrs."

While the principal purpose of at-home cards is to let people know your new address, when sent with announcements they can also let people know that you have chosen to continue using your maiden name. Your name appears on the first line followed by your husband's name on line two. The remainder of the card reads as it normally would. Since you could have presented yourself as "Mrs." but did not, it will be assumed that you are still using your maiden name.

At-home cards are like the change-of-address cards you might send when you move. They simply announce your new address and are a great convenience for anyone who wants to keep in touch with you. They are not gift-request cards and should never be interpreted as such.

Mr. and Mrs. Antonio Marc Velez

After the first of December

3675 Marbury Road
Fort Worth, Texas 76133

Sample of an at-home card

Sample of a direction card

From the Cincinnatian Hotel to Ault Park Pavilion

TURN ONTO VINE STREET, THEN RIGHT ONTO US-22.
TAKE RAMP ONTO I-71 NORTH.
AT EXIT 6, TURN RIGHT ONTO SR-561 (EDWARDS ROAD).
TURN LEFT ONTO OBSERVATORY AVENUE.
FOLLOW SIGNS TO THE PAVILION.

From Ault Park Pavilion to Maketewah Country Club

EXIT THE PARK ON OBSERVATORY AVENUE.
TURN RIGHT ONTO SR-561 (EDWARDS ROAD).
TAKE RAMP ONTO I-71 NORTH.
AT EXIT 7, TURN RIGHT ONTO SR-562.
TURN RIGHT ON US-42 (READING ROAD).
THE COUNTRY CLUB IS LE
AT 5401 READING ROAD.

The honour of your presence is requested

at the marriage ceremony

Friday evening, the fifth of October

at six o'clock

First Presbyterian Church

Philadelphia, Pennsylvania

Sample of a
ceremony card

Please present this card

at All Saints' Episcopal Church

Saturday, the fifteenth of September

Pew number _____

Sample of a pew card

Direction and Map Cards

Out-of-town guests will appreciate receiving a direction card or map card. Direction cards give simple yet explicit driving instructions to your wedding, while map cards are maps with the routes to your wedding highlighted. Map cards generally feature major roads and landmarks to help your guests find their way. When direction cards or map cards are included, the street address does not appear on the invitations.

As with other enclosures, direction cards and map cards should complement the wedding invitations. They typically match the invitation style and color. To make them easier to read, a sans serif (block) lettering style is usually used.

Direction cards and map cards are usually sent with the wedding invitations but may be sent afterward in an envelope or as a postcard to those who accept your invitation. When sent afterward, a line reading "We are looking forward to having you attend" may be added to the top of the cards.

Ceremony Cards

For large receptions with small, private ceremonies, invitations are sent to the reception. Guests invited to the ceremony are sent smaller ceremony cards enclosed with their reception invitations. The same size as reception cards, ceremony cards serve as invitations to the ceremony. They are usually designed to match the reception invitation but they may be handwritten when the guest list is small.

The wording "request the honour of your presence" is used when the ceremony is held in a church while "request the pleasure of your company" is used when it is held elsewhere. Both "marriage ceremony" and "wedding ceremony" are proper. Whichever word ("marriage" or "wedding") is used on the reception invitations must be repeated on the ceremony card.

Accommodations Cards

Accommodations cards are enclosed with the invitations sent to out-of-town guests who are unfamiliar with the area and need to make hotel reservations. They list the names and phone numbers of nearby hotels. If you are paying for your guests' rooms, a notation to that effect is made on the cards.

Within-the-Ribbon Cards

Pews may be cordoned off with white ribbons or cords to indicate a special seating section. When this is done, small cards reading "Within the ribbon" are sent with the invitations to those guests who will be seated in that section. The guests then bring the cards to the ceremony, which enables the ushers to seat them in the appropriate section.

Pew Cards

Pew cards are used when specific pews have been assigned for some or all of the guests. This helps the ushers efficiently guide their guests to their assigned seats. Pew cards are sent with the invitations. A space on the card is filled in by hand with the appropriate pew.

Admission Cards

Admission cards are a lot like tickets to the theater or to a ball game—you need to present them to gain admittance. Admission cards are generally used by well-known people who want to make sure that only invited guests are allowed to attend their wedding. They are sent with the invitations to all guests and may be personalized.

Transportation Cards

When a large number of out-of-town guests are attending a wedding, especially one in a big city, transportation from the wedding to the reception is occasionally provided. Sent with the invitations, transportation cards let your

• POINTS OF STYLE •

The Flap Over the Flap

Traditionally the return address was blind-embossed or engraved on the envelope flap. Blind-embossing is the more traditional of the two and was preferred over engraving because of the feeling that the first time guests see engraving, it should be on the invitations. The return address, on the other hand, should melt into the background.

guests know that their local travel plans have been taken care of. The cards generally read "Transportation will be provided / from the ceremony to the reception."

PREPARING INVITATIONS FOR MAILING

Addressing the Envelopes

Wedding invitations were once delivered by hand. If you were a bride back in those days, your footman delivered your invitations to your guests' homes. Their servants received the invitations and removed them from their outer envelope, an envelope much too pedestrian for your guests to handle themselves. The servants then presented the invitation to your guests in its pristine inside envelope. Because the invitations were already at their destination, the inside envelopes had only the names of your guests written on them. The address was no longer needed. They just had to be directed to the appropriate members of the household.

Following tradition, wedding invitations are still sometimes sent in two envelopes. The outside envelope is the mailing envelope. The mailing envelopes have glue on them; the inside envelopes do not and they are also a bit smaller. Your guests' names and addresses are written on the mailing envelope. Except for "Mr." and Mrs.," abbreviations are not used on the mailing envelope. Spell out honorifics, ranks, and titles unless the name is too long to fit on one line. Use the spelled-out forms for "Street," "Avenue," "Apartment," etc. Similarly, "Rural Route" and "Post Office Box" are always written out.

Your guests' names are repeated on the inside envelope. This time, however, only their titles and surnames are used. If children under the age of eighteen are invited, their first names would appear on the line beneath their parents' names.

The back flap of the outside envelope bears the sender's address.

While you may use any color ink you please to address your envelopes, you want to be certain the handwriting is neat and legible. Many couples choose to retain a calligrapher to address their invitations. If a calligrapher is not a viable alternative and your handwriting is not the best, you may consider running the envelopes through your computer printer. There are a number of suitably elegant typefaces for the job.

Addressing the Envelopes

	OUTSIDE ENVELOPE	INSIDE ENVELOPE
MARRIED COUPLE	Mr. and Mrs. Troy Clayton	Mr. and Mrs. Clayton
WITH CHILDREN UNDER EIGHTEEN LIVING AT HOME*	Mr. and Mrs. Troy Clayton	Mr. and Mrs. Clayton Marvin and Heather

* The name of the oldest child is listed first followed by the names of his or her siblings in reverse chronological order.

	OUTSIDE ENVELOPE	INSIDE ENVELOPE
WITH CHILDREN OVER EIGHTEEN LIVING AT HOME*	Miss Heather Clayton OR Mr. Marvin Clayton	Miss Clayton OR Mr. Clayton

* Children over the age of eighteen should each receive a separate invitation.

	OUTSIDE ENVELOPE	INSIDE ENVELOPE
IN WHICH WOMAN KEPT MAIDEN NAME	Ms. Christine Pritchett and Mr. Troy Clayton	Ms. Pritchett and Mr. Clayton
IN WHICH MAN IS A DOCTOR	Doctor and Mrs. Troy Clayton	Doctor and Mrs. Clayton
IN WHICH BOTH ARE DOCTORS	Doctor Christine Clayton and Doctor Troy Clayton	Doctor Clayton and Doctor Clayton OR The Doctors Clayton
IN WHICH WOMAN IS A DOCTOR	Doctor Christine Clayton and Mr. Troy Clayton OR Mr. and Mrs. Troy Clayton	Doctor Clayton and Mr. Clayton OR Mr. and Mrs. Clayton
IN WHICH MAN IS A JUDGE	The Honorable Troy Clayton and Mrs. Clayton	Judge and Mrs. Clayton
IN WHICH WOMAN IS A JUDGE	The Honorable Christine Clayton and Mr. Troy Clayton	Judge Clayton and Mr. Clayton
IN WHICH BOTH ARE LAWYERS	Mr. and Mrs. Troy Clayton	Mr. and Mrs. Clayton

UNMARRIED COUPLE LIVING TOGETHER	Miss Christine Pritchett Mr. Troy Clayton OR Ms. Christine Pritchett Mr. Troy Clayton	Miss Pritchett Mr. Clayton OR Ms. Pritchett Mr. Clayton
IF TWO PEOPLE LIVE TOGETHER, USE DIFFERENT SURNAMES, BUT PRESENT THEMSELVES AS A COUPLE, YOU MAY CHOOSE TO USE THE FORMAT FOR A MARRIED COUPLE.	Ms. Christine Pritchett and Mr. Troy Clayton Ms. Christine Pritchett and Ms. Kimberly Kelleher Mr. Troy Clayton and Mr. Peter Madison	Ms. Pritchett and Mr. Clayton Ms. Pritchett and Ms. Kelleher Mr. Clayton and Mr. Madison
DIVORCED WOMAN	Ms. Christine Pritchett Clayton OR Mrs. Christine Pritchett Clayton	Ms. Clayton OR Mrs. Clayton
WHO HAS RESUMED USING MAIDEN NAME	Ms. Christine Pritchett	Ms. Pritchett
WIDOW	Mrs. Troy Clayton	Mrs. Clayton
SINGLE WOMAN*	Ms. Christine Pritchett OR Miss Christine Pritchett	Ms. Pritchett OR Miss Pritchett
AND DATE	Ms. Christine Pritchett OR Miss Christine Pritchett	Ms. Pritchett and escort OR Ms. Pritchett and guest Miss Pritchett and escort OR Miss Pritchett and guest

Traditionally, an unmarried woman is addressed as "Miss." However, with the decline of the use of the honorific "Miss" by young women, you may decide on a case-by-case basis whether "Ms." is more appropriate for your guest.

SINGLE MAN	Mr. Troy Clayton	Mr. Clayton
AND DATE*	Mr. Troy Clayton	Mr. Clayton and guest

* See page 105 for more on inviting guests.

Addressing the Envelopes: MILITARY COUPLES

	OUTSIDE ENVELOPE	INSIDE ENVELOPE
MARRIED COUPLE IN WHICH THE MAN IS AN OFFICER	Colonel Troy Clayton and Mrs. Clayton	Colonel and Mrs. Clayton
IN WHICH THE WOMAN IS AN OFFICER	Colonel Christine Clayton and Mr. Troy Clayton	Colonel Clayton and Mr. Clayton
IN WHICH BOTH ARE OFFICERS*	Colonel Christine Clayton and Colonel Troy Clayton	Colonel Clayton and Colonel Clayton

* If the officers are of different ranks, list the name of the higher-ranking officer first regardless of gender. If the guests have the same rank, list the woman first.

	OUTSIDE ENVELOPE	INSIDE ENVELOPE
IN WHICH ONE OR BOTH ARE RETIRED OFFICERS	Forms are the same as for active-duty officers.	Forms are the same as for active-duty officers.
IN WHICH THE MAN IS A NONCOMMISSIONED OFFICER OR ENLISTED MAN*	Sergeant Major Troy Clayton and Mrs. Clayton OR Mr. and Mrs. Troy Clayton	Sergeant Major and Mrs. Clayton OR Mr. and Mrs. Clayton
IN WHICH THE WOMAN IS A NONCOMMISSIONED OFFICER OR ENLISTED WOMAN*	Sergeant Major Christine Clayton and Mr. Troy Clayton OR Mr. and Mrs. Troy Clayton	Sergeant Major Clayton and Mr. Clayton OR Mr. and Mrs. Clayton

* Depending on the situation and personal preference, noncommissioned officers and enlisted personnel may or may not use their ranks socially. Check for the preference of the individual service member. Also see Military Weddings, page 76.

	OUTSIDE ENVELOPE	INSIDE ENVELOPE
IN WHICH BOTH ARE NONCOMMISSIONED OFFICERS OR ENLISTED PERSONNEL*	(Rank/Rating) Christine Clayton and (Rank/Rating) Troy Clayton OR Mr. and Mrs. Troy Clayton	(Rank/Rating) Clayton and (Rank/Rating) Clayton OR Mr. and Mrs. Clayton

* If the guests have different ranks or ratings, list the person with the higher rank or rating first regardless of gender. If the guests have the same rank or rating, list the woman first.

SINGLE WOMAN WHO IS AN OFFICER	Captain Christine Pritchett	Captain Pritchett
WHO IS A NONCOMMISSIONED OFFICER OR ENLISTED WOMAN	(Rating) Christine Pritchett OR Ms. Christine Pritchett	(Rating) Pritchett OR Ms. Pritchett
SINGLE MAN WHO IS AN OFFICER	Captain Troy Clayton	Captain Clayton
WHO IS A NONCOMMISSIONED OFFICER OR ENLISTED WOMAN	(Rating) Troy Clayton OR Mr. Troy Clayton	(Rating) Clayton OR Mr. Clayton

· POINTS OF STYLE ·
Personalized Stamps

Thanks to modern technology, even your postage stamp can be customized to match your wedding invitation. Working with the U.S. Postal Service or other online services, you can upload images, including motifs from your invitation or photos, to bring a personal touch to the outside of your invitation envelope. Customized stamps are also a popular choice for save-the-date cards and thank-you notes.

One word of caution: With some printers, the inside envelope, which is often on a heavier stock than the outside envelope and is lined, will prove too thick to run through the printer. Because the style of lettering on the inside and outside envelopes needs to match, this technical challenge may eliminate this option for you.

Only the address appears on the outside envelope flap. The names do not. The apartment number must be given when applicable, since without the name there would be no way of identifying the sender. The apartment may appear alone on the first line with "Apartment" spelled out or at the end of the street address, preceded by a comma or a bullet. (A bullet is a period that is raised to a point halfway between the top and bottom of a line.)

The address of whoever issued the invitations appears on the back flap. If, for example, your parents issued your invitations, their address appears. Many people, however, use the return address as an indication where the gifts should be sent, so if you would like to have your presents sent directly to you, you may use your address for the return address.

Invitations to Siblings Under the Age of Eighteen

When addressing envelopes to two or more siblings under the age of eighteen who are living at home, the name of the oldest child is listed first followed by the names of his or her siblings in reverse chronological order. If they are over eighteen, they receive separate invitations.

Addressing Envelopes to Families with Children

Wedding invitations are sent to the adult members of the household. In this case, the outside envelope is addressed to the parents who receive the invitations on behalf of their children. Their children's names (not "and family"), if you wish to invite them, are written on the inside envelope on a line beneath the names of their parents.

The Use of "Junior"

If "junior" is a part of a man's name, you would include it (or "Jr.") on the outside envelope. It is not necessary to repeat it on the inside envelope unless both "junior" and "senior" are living at the same address.

Numerals

Numerals are usually used for the street number, although it is also appropriate to write out numbers one through twenty. Numbered streets may appear whichever way is more aesthetically pleasing. Numerals are always used for zip codes.

Invitations to Unmarried Couples Living Together

The woman's name should appear on the first line and the man's on the second. For same-sex couples, the names may be ordered alphabetically or to your own preference.

Invitations for Dating Couples

The nicest way to invite dates is to call your friends, get the names of their dates, and send them each an invitation. A less formal way is to address the inside envelopes with either "Mr. Clayton and guest" or "Miss Clayton and escort." Women who feel that an escort is unnecessary in this day and age prefer "Miss Clayton and guest" or "Ms. Clayton and guest."

Assembling the Invitation

Your wedding invitations may arrive already stuffed into their inner envelopes or in separate stacks of invitations, enclosure cards, and inner and outer envelopes. If yours come unassembled, there is no need to panic. Assembling wedding invitations is really quite simple, albeit time consuming.

A single-fold invitation
inserted into an envelope

Inserting a single-fold invitation
with an enclosure card

A two-fold invitation
inserted into an envelope

Inserting a two-fold invitation
with an enclosure card

Enclosing a reply card
and envelope

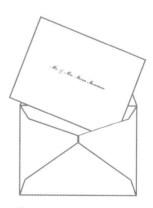

Placing an inner envelope
into an outer envelope

For the most part, wedding invitations are assembled in size order. The invitation itself is first. The enclosure cards are stacked on top of the invitations, not inside. The reception card is placed on top of the invitation. Then the reply envelope is placed face down on the reception card. The reply card is slipped face up beneath the flap of the reply envelope. These are the most frequently used enclosures. Any other enclosures are added face up in size order (usually at-home card, direction card, accommodations card, pew card, etc.).

The single-fold invitation and its enclosures are placed into the inside envelope with the fold of the invitation at the bottom of the envelope and the engraving facing the back of the envelope. You can tell whether or not you stuffed the envelope correctly by removing the invitation with your right hand. If you can read the invitation without turning it, it was stuffed correctly.

The procedure for assembling traditional invitations (those with a second fold) is similar. The enclosures are placed on top of the lower half of the invitation's face in the same order described above. The invitation is folded from top to bottom over the enclosures. The invitation is then placed into the inside envelope with the fold toward the bottom of the envelope. As with other invitations, traditional invitations are correctly stuffed when they can be read without being turned, after being removed from the envelope with your right hand.

Once stuffed, the inside envelopes are inserted into the outside envelopes. The front of the inside envelope faces the back of the outside envelope.

Using Tissues

All wedding invitations were once shipped with small pieces of tissue separating each invitation. This prevented the slow-drying ink from smudging. Before mailing her invitations, the bride removed the tissues, as they were merely packing material and served no point of etiquette. Through the years, many brides, unaware of the impropriety of sending tissued invitations, left the tissues in. As this practice grew, tissued invitations became as proper as non-tissued invitations.

Today, wedding invitations are properly sent both ways. Tissues are starting to serve an important function again as the postal service's sorting equipment can cause smudging on invitations sent without tissues. If you are

RECEPTION INVITATION:

Mr. and Mrs. Andrew Jay Forrester

request the pleasure of your company

at the marriage reception of their daughter

Jennifer Marie

and

Mr. Nicholas Jude Strickland

Saturday, the twenty-third of August

at seven o'clock

Sleepy Hollow Country Club

Scarborough, New York

CEREMONY CARD:

The honour of your presence is requested

at the marriage ceremony

Saturday, the twenty-third of August

at six o'clock

Church of Christ

Bedford, New York

sending invitations without tissues, you may be able to ask your local post office to hand-cancel them. Hand-canceling also prevents the postal service from printing their advertising, disguised as part of the cancellation mark, on your wedding invitations.

Since the tissues are meant to prevent smudging, they should be placed over the copy on each invitation and enclosure.

Mailing Your Invitation

Wedding invitations should be mailed four to six weeks before the wedding. For summer and holiday weddings, many brides mail their invitations eight weeks before the wedding since people are more likely to be traveling at those times.

The invitation's size and the number of enclosure cards affect the postage. To determine the correct postage, you should have your invitations (including the stamp on the reply envelope) weighed at the post office from which they will be sent.

RECEPTION INVITATIONS

Invitations to the Reception

On occasion a couple may choose to have a small, intimate wedding ceremony with only the closest of family and friends in attendance, followed by a larger reception. Since more people are invited to the reception than the ceremony, the invitations are for the reception.

Reception invitations always "request the pleasure of your company" since the reception is not being held in a house of worship. The word "and" is used to join the names of the bride and groom. The phrases "marriage reception" and "wedding reception" are both correct. "Marriage reception" is the more traditional of the two but many couples prefer "wedding reception," arguing that a wedding is the act of getting married while marriage is the result of that decision.

The same rules regarding the sequence of wording, use of social titles, addressing the envelopes, etc. that apply to wedding invitations also apply to reception invitations.

An invitation to a reception is also sent to those guests who will be attending the ceremony. The invitation to the ceremony is either extended orally or through a ceremony card included with the reception invitation (see page 97).

Late Receptions

Wedding receptions take place on the day of the wedding. Any reception occurring after that date is not properly referred to as a wedding reception. Rather, it is a party or reception in honor of the recently married couple. As such, it requires a separate invitation and a separate mailing. Invitations are never properly sent with announcements.

These receptions are held for a variety of reasons. Most late receptions are held when the bride and her family live in different parts of the country. Others, especially those involving older couples or second-time brides, may hold late receptions due to professional considerations. Whatever the reasons, late receptions are becoming a more common occurrence.

Invitations to a late reception contain a line reading "in honour of" or "in honor of" followed on a separate line with the names of the couple.

Mr. and Mrs. Andrew Jay Forrester

request the pleasure of your company

at the dinner reception

in honour of

Mr. and Mrs. Nicholas Jude Strickland

Saturday, the twentieth of September

at seven o'clock

Sleepy Hollow Country Club

Scarborough, New York

REVISING AN ISSUED
ANNOUNCEMENT OR INVITATION

Postponement of a Wedding

Weddings are occasionally postponed due to illness or an unexpected death in the family. If you have not yet mailed your invitations, you may include a small card informing your guests of the new date. If your invitation has already been mailed, an announcement should be prepared and mailed immediately. If time does not permit for printing and mailing in a timely manner (i.e. to arrive at least two weeks before the wedding), your guests may be notified of the new date by phone.

POSTPONEMENT ANNOUNCEMENT:

Mr. and Mrs. Andrew Jay Forrester

announce that the marriage of their daughter

Jennifer Marie

to

Mr. Nicholas Jude Strickland

has been postponed to

Saturday, the twentieth of September

at six o'clock

Church of Christ

Bedford, New York

Recalling Wedding Invitations

Wedding invitations are recalled when a wedding needs to be postponed before a new wedding date has been set. Recalling invitations officially cancels them so new invitations must be issued to re-invite your guests once a new date has been set.

The reason that the invitations are being recalled is usually mentioned. If there is not enough time to send recall notices so that your guests may change their plans without great inconvenience or cost, you may notify them by phone.

RECALL NOTICE:

Mr. and Mrs. Andrew Jay Forrester

regret that the illness of their daughter

Jennifer Marie

obliges them to recall their invitations

to her marriage to

Mr. Nicholas Jude Strickland

on Saturday, the twenty-third of September

NEW INVITATION:

Mr. and Mrs. Andrew Jay Forrester

announce that the wedding of their daughter

Jennifer Marie

to

Mr. Nicholas Jude Strickland

which was postponed, will now take place

on Saturday, the twenty-third of October

etc.

Canceling a Wedding

When a wedding needs to be canceled, formal announcements may be sent. If there is not enough time to send a formal announcement, phone calls may be made instead.

WEDDING CANCELLATION:

Mr. and Mrs. Andrew Jay Forrester

are obliged to recall their invitation

to the marriage of their daughter

Jennifer Marie

to

Mr. Nicholas Jude Strickland

as the marriage will not take place

RESPONSIBILITIES OF THE GROOM'S FAMILY

While the bride's family is traditionally responsible for issuing the bulk of the correspondence surrounding the wedding, the groom and his family also have their roles and responsibilities. As the groom's family would like to be informed and included in any decisions relating to their son's wedding, they should also advise the bride's family before issuing any invitations or announcements related to the wedding.

Invitations to an Engagement Party

Engagement parties are often hosted by the bride's parents. If it is more practical for the groom's parents to host a party, they may do so instead. The invitations say that the event is being held in honor of the couple, although they do not usually mention that it is in honor of the engagement. The guests will undoubtedly figure it out on their own.

Mr. and Mrs. Andrew Jay Forrester

request the pleasure of your company

at a dinner in honour of

Miss Jennifer Marie Forrester

and Mr. Nicholas Jude Strickland

Friday, the thirtieth of March

at seven o'clock

2830 Meadowbrook Drive

Bedford, New York

If your engagement is being announced at an engagement party, neither your name nor your fiancé's should appear on the invitation, as that would likely give away the surprise. The invitations read as though they are not for any special event other than to enjoy the company of family and good friends.

Engagement Party Hosted by Friends of the Parents

When an engagement party is hosted by friends of your parents, the invitations are issued by your parents' friends so their names appear on the first line of the invitation. Your parents' names are not mentioned.

Invitations to Meet You or Your Fiancé

In lieu of an engagement party or in addition to an engagement party hosted by the bride's parents, a party to meet you or your fiancé may be in order. If, for example, the bride's parents held an engagement party in New York and your parents in California want to host a party as well, they may host a party "to meet" the bride. This party gives your family and friends an opportunity to get to know the bride before the wedding. The party is in the bride's honor and the invitations should allude to that.

To meet

Miss Jennifer Marie Forrester

Mr. and Mrs. John Peter Strickland

request the pleasure of your company

at a cocktail reception

Friday, the sixth of March

at eight o'clock

910 Oakland Drive

San Marino, California

Mr. and Mrs. John Peter Strickland

request the pleasure of your company

at the rehearsal dinner

in honour of

Miss Jennifer Marie Forrester

and

Mr. Nicholas Jude Strickland

Friday, the twenty-second of August

at half after seven o'clock

Tappan Hill

Tarrytown, New York

Sample rehearsal dinner invitations

Nellie and John Strickland

request the pleasure of your company

at the rehearsal dinner for

jen & nick

Friday, August 22nd

at 7:30pm

Tappan Hill

Tarrytown, New York

Wedding Invitations Issued by the Groom's Parents

On rare occasions, perhaps when the bride's parents are deceased or when they live in a foreign country, the groom's parents may issue the wedding invitations. The format is a little different from the standard format. The parents' relationship to the groom is mentioned on the fifth line of the invitation instead of on the third line. This way, the invitations can still be read as the bride being married to the groom. Both the bride and the groom use their full names, preceded by their titles.

Mr. and Mrs. John Peter Strickland

request the pleasure of your company

at the marriage of

Miss Jennifer Marie Forrester

to their son

Mr. Nicholas Jude Strickland

etc.

Rehearsal Dinner Invitations

Custom suggests that the groom's parents host the rehearsal dinner and, therefore, issue its invitations. The rehearsal dinner takes place on the night before the wedding and is given as a courtesy to the bride's family. The rehearsal dinner invitations are usually worded formally, but many times just first names are used. This less formal style can be a way to let guests know how you, your fiancé, and your fiancé's parents wish to be addressed.

Traditionally, the rehearsal dinner was held for just the wedding party in order to get them fed after the rehearsal—and to give the bride's mother one less responsibility. While many rehearsal dinners are still reserved for the wedding party, others have expanded to include the wedding party, their spouses or dates, and out-of-town guests.

Engraved invitations are rarely used for rehearsal dinners any more. Other printing options, such as thermography and even home printers, produce attractive invitations at a much more reasonable cost.

While invitations to the rehearsal dinner should reflect the nature of the event, they should not compete with or upstage the wedding invitation. Rehearsal dinner invitations should be sent two weeks before the wedding.

CHAPTER FIVE

Invitations to Social Occasions

Invitations to social occasions may be formal, informal, or anything in between. The invitation that you send sets the tone for your event and helps your guests determine appropriate dress. The formality of your invitations should match the formality of your event.

Your invitations may be engraved, thermographed, or produced on a home printer. Engraving is the more formal and elegant option while thermography is a little less formal and less expensive. Home printing is certainly the most economical and, with a quality printer, can produce acceptable results for more casual occasions.

Invitations for formal events are generally engraved on white or ecru (ivory or buff) cards, generally in black ink. Invitations to less formal events, like a cookout, may be printed on correspondence cards with bright-colored borders with matching lined envelopes. The lettering may be fun and fashionable. This is your opportunity to be as creative as your imagination allows.

Whether formal or not, the composition of your invitations contains the same basic elements. In other words, while the rules of etiquette for informal invitations are not as strict as those for formal invitations, the same information must be included, for example, host, event, date, time, and place.

While it is impossible to include examples of every type of invitation that you might send, you can easily come up with your own wording by looking at the four samples provided and substituting your own information for the information in the sample. For example, if you were hosting a dinner dance celebrating your parents' anniversary, you could follow the format of Sample #2 on page 121 substituting your names on the invitation line, "dinner dance" for "cocktails and dinner" on the event line, and by adding "in honour of," "the fortieth wedding anniversary of," and your parents' names on the subsequent lines.

The order in which your information appears is not necessarily dictated by convention. You may wish to afford your guest of honor more distinction. You can do this by moving his name from the body of the invitation to the top. Notice that Samples #1 and #3 have identical information.

In Sample #4, the event is more casual and so is the wording.

As you will see, all four sample invitations have varying degrees of formality yet carry the same basic information. When you compose your invitations, follow one of the samples (or create your own format) and simply make sure that you include all the necessary information.

SAMPLE #1:

Invitation Line	*Mr. and Mrs. Stephen Julian Hameroff*
Request Line	*request the pleasure of your company*
Event Line #1	*at a cocktail party*
Event Line #2	*to meet*
Event Line #3	*Mrs. David Allen Meppen*
Date Line	*Saturday, the fifteenth of June*
Time Line	*at seven o'clock*
Address Line	*The Warwick Hotel*
City and State Line	*Houston, Texas*
Reply Request Line	*The favour of a reply is requested*

SAMPLE #2:

Invitation Line	*Mr. and Mrs. Stephen Julian Hameroff*
Request Line	*request the pleasure of your company*
Event Line #1	*at a dinner dance*
Event Line #2	*in honour of*
Event Line #3	*the fortieth wedding anniversary of*
Event Line #4	*Mr. and Mrs. David Allen Meppen*
Date Line	*Saturday, the fifteenth of June*
Time Line	*at seven o'clock*
Address Line	*The Warwick Hotel*
City and State Line	*Houston, Texas*
Reply Request Line	*The favour of a reply is requested*

SAMPLE #3:

Event Line #2	*To meet*
Event Line #3	*Mrs. David Allen Meppen*
Invitation Line	*Mr. and Mrs. Stephen Julian Hameroff*
Request Line	*request the pleasure of your company*
Event Line #1	*at a cocktail party*
Date Line	*Saturday, the fifteenth of June*
Time Line	*at seven o'clock*
Address Line	*The Warwick Hotel*
City and State Line	*Houston, Texas*
Reply Request Line	*The favour of a reply is requested*

SAMPLE #4:

Invitation Line	*Debbie and Steve Hameroff*
Request Line	*invite you to*
Event Line	*a pool party and barbeque*
Date Line	*Saturday, June 15th*
Time Line	*at 1:00*
Address Line	*2126 Lazy Lane*
City and State Line	*Houston, Texas*
Reply Request Line	*Please reply*

INVITATIONS TO A FORMAL DINNER

Invitations to large, formal dinners used to be engraved on ecru or white letter sheets. Today, the preference is for engraving on heavyweight card stock.

Correspondence cards (flat, heavy, single cards) are occasionally used as well, but they are considered much less formal.

Black ink is the color of choice for formal invitations, but any conservative ink color will make a tasteful invitation.

The most formal invitations leave a space for your guests' names to be handwritten or calligraphed. (See sample at right.) This format gives special honor to your guests. When wording an invitation to dinner, it is important to remember that guests are invited "at a dinner" or "to a dinner," never "for dinner" unless they are being served as the entrée.

INVITATIONS TO A DINNER TO HONOR A GUEST

Invitations that honor a guest follow the same guidelines as for formal dinners; however, the honoree's name appears on the invitation. The honoree's name may appear in the body of the invitation or at the top.

These invitations differ from wedding invitations, in that the American spelling of "honor" is used instead of "honour." The same is true with the word "favor."

Samples of dinner invitations

Mr. and Mrs. Jeffrey Harris Atkinson

request the pleasure of the company of

Mr. and Mrs. Charles Winn Montgomery

at dinner

Friday, the eighteenth of November

at eight o'clock

922 Club Creek

Grosse Pointe Farms, Michigan

IN HONOR OF

ADMIRAL WILLIAM STANTON TAGG

MR. AND MRS. ARTHUR DAVID LINCOLN

REQUEST THE PLEASURE OF YOUR COMPANY

AT DINNER

THURSDAY, THE TENTH OF OCTOBER

AT EIGHT O'CLOCK

1825 SYCAMORE LANE

CHARLESTON, SOUTH CAROLINA

INVITATIONS TO MEET A GUEST

Invitations to meet a guest are extended when the hosts wish to introduce somebody to their friends, family, and associates. The party might be held to meet a celebrity, someone new in the area, or, perhaps, your daughter's fiancé. The guidelines follow those for invitations to honor a guest.

To meet

Miss Kimberly Ann Keleher

Mr. and Mrs. Peter Thomas Madison

request the pleasure of your company

for cocktails

Wednesday, the second of April

at seven o'clock

4209 Granada Boulevard

Coral Gables, Florida

Sample of an invitation to meet a guest

GOVERNMENT AND DIPLOMATIC INVITATIONS

The most formal invitations issued by government officials and diplomats are engraved in black ink on white or ecru stock. However, government invitations exhibit all the creativity and variety of styles seen in the private sector.

In the United States, "the Honorable" is a courtesy title used with current and retired high-ranking federal and state officials and judges, and with some local officials. As a general rule, those appointed by the president of the United States and approved by the Senate, and anyone elected to public office are entitled to be addressed as "the Honorable" for life. As a courtesy title, "the Honorable" describes an individual: This person is honorable. As such, it never precedes just the name of an office.

Others use "the Honorable" when addressing the officeholder. "The Honorable" is always used before a full name. Use "the Honorable" when addressing an envelope, in a letter's heading, or when introducing an official to a group. "The Honorable" is not used in a salutation or in conversation. In the United States it is not used on an invitation's inside envelope or on place cards.

While others address an officeholder as "the Honorable," an officeholder never uses "the Honorable" with his or her own name. So an invitation is issued in just the officeholder's name or by the name of the office.

The Mayor of Flint
requests the pleasure of your company
at luncheon for
The Mayor of Flint, Chester, United Kingdom
and Mrs. Hollywell
Thursday, the fifth of May
One o'clock
Flint Club
140 East Second Street
Flint, Michigan

Benjamin Carper Holmes
United States Senator for Mississippi
requests the pleasure of your company
at a Holiday Open House
Friday, the seventeenth of December
Russell Senate Office Building
Room 325
from four to six o'clock

R.S.V.P.   Constitution and Delaware Avenues
(202) 555-5678   Washington

In the diplomatic arena, special attention is paid to names and the proper wording of invitations. There are more than 200 governmental entities; each has its own unique structure and hierarchy. While similarities exist, each has its own traditions. Thus, to assure the most successful outcome, it is important to check for the preference of the bearer with your contact in his or her organization or the protocol officer at his or her embassy or consulate to find the tradition of a country.

To honor
His Highness Sheikh Mohammad Bin Rashid Al Maktoum

Ambassador Norman McGill Henderson
and Mrs. Henderson
request the pleasure of your company
at a reception
Wednesday, the twelfth of May
at six o'clock
Diplomatic Reception Rooms
Department of State

R.S.V.P.   2201 C Street, Northwest
(202) 555-5678   Washington

PARTY INVITATIONS

Invitations to informal parties should reflect the nature of the event. They may be festive, lighthearted, or conservative. The choice of format, paper color, ink, motifs, and language all help to set the tone.

Invitations to informal gatherings can be produced on a quality home printer. Often referred to as imprintables, these invitations are purchased with a pre-printed design, frame, or embossing, providing you maximum flexibility in creating the appropriate wording for the event.

Samples of
informal party invitations

Billings & Ashbridge
Jewelers, Silversmiths, Stationers

Announces the opening of its new

1700 West Fifth Street
Greenville, North Carolina 27834

705 559 1212
www.BillingsAshbridge.com

An Evening Under the Stars

Please join us for
cocktails, dinner, and dancing
Friday, the eleventh of September
at seven o'clock
Bayview Yacht Club
Tampa, Florida

Lilyan and Robert Stowe

DANCE INVITATIONS

Dance invitations follow the same format as formal invitations. The event may be mentioned in the body of the invitation by using either "at a small dance" or "at a ball." It may also be mentioned in the lower right-hand corner simply as "Dancing."

Mr. and Mrs. Stephen James McGee
request the pleasure of your company
at a small dance
Saturday, the sixth of November
at ten o'clock in the evening
The Waldorf-Astoria
New York City

R.s.v.p.
1040 Fifth Avenue
New York, New York 10021

Mr. and Mrs. Stephen James McGee
request the pleasure of your company
Saturday, the sixth of November
at ten o'clock in the evening
The Waldorf-Astoria
New York City

R.s.v.p.
1040 Fifth Avenue
New York, New York 10021   Dancing

LUNCHEON INVITATIONS

Invitations to a luncheon may be formal or informal depending on the nature of the event. If formal, black ink engraved on white or ecru cards is preferred. Pre-engraved fill-in invitations may be used for formal, yet smaller, luncheons. More casual luncheons can be printed on colored paper, with a motif or design element that conveys the spirit of the gathering, and, if the guest list is small, printed using a home or office printer.

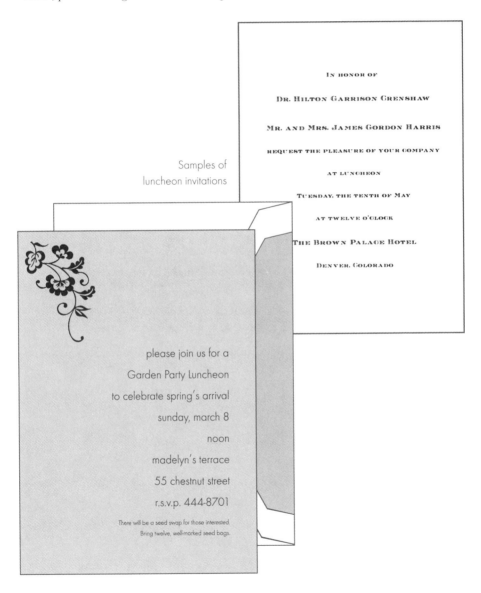

Samples of
luncheon invitations

IN HONOR OF

DR. HILTON GARRISON CRENSHAW

MR. AND MRS. JAMES GORDON HARRIS

REQUEST THE PLEASURE OF YOUR COMPANY

AT LUNCHEON

TUESDAY, THE TENTH OF MAY

AT TWELVE O'CLOCK

THE BROWN PALACE HOTEL

DENVER, COLORADO

please join us for a
Garden Party Luncheon
to celebrate spring's arrival
sunday, march 8
noon
madelyn's terrace
55 chestnut street
r.s.v.p. 444-8701

There will be a seed swap for those interested.
Bring twelve, well-marked seed bags.

INVITATIONS TO A TEA

Teas are an ideal way to host a large group of people in a less expensive manner than a sit-down dinner. Often held for occasions such as bridal showers, baby showers, or to honor a guest, teas are typically held in the afternoon, between two and five, with traditional "high tea" time being five o'clock.

Invitations to tea are mailed at least ten days in advance. They may be professionally printed or engraved or produced on a home printer, depending on the formality of the tea.

Please join us for a

Baby Shower Tea Party

in honor of
Mother-to-be-of-twins

Martha MacGregor

Saturday, April 4, 2009
Two o'clock
Scallions Restaurant
44 Lake Avenue
Saratoga Springs, New York
Please respond to Jennifer Spangenberg at 555-8701 by April 1

Samples of
tea invitations

MRS. JOHN LELAND KENSINGTON

REQUESTS THE PLEASURE OF YOUR COMPANY

AT A TEA

TUESDAY, THE THIRTEENTH OF SEPTEMBER

FROM FOUR UNTIL SIX O'CLOCK

1776 STONE DRIVE

BIRMINGHAM, ALABAMA

WEDDING ANNIVERSARIES

While wedding anniversaries are observed every year, major celebrations are usually reserved for the twenty-fifth, fortieth, and fiftieth anniversaries. While some traditional color guidelines may be followed in choosing an invitation—silver for a twenty-fifth anniversary, gold for a fiftieth—there are no hard and fast rules for choosing paper stock or ink. Invitation styles vary dramatically depending on the individuals being celebrated and the nature of the event. An invitation that best captures the spirit of the couple or the theme of the event makes for the best choice.

Invitations to wedding anniversaries are usually extended by the couple's children and their spouses, but often friends, grandchildren, and even the couple themselves, may issue them as well. The years of the marriage are typically shown at the top of the invitation. Depending upon the format of the invitation, reply information may be included on the invitation or on a separate reply card.

1961-2011

Mr. and Mrs. Nicholas Jude Strickland, junior

Mr. and Mrs. Robert Stuart Strickland

Mr. and Mrs. John Kevin Murphy

request the pleasure of your company

at a dinner to celebrate

the Fiftieth Wedding Anniversary of

Mr. and Mrs. Nicholas Jude Strickland

Saturday, the second of April

at seven o'clock

Sleepy Hollow Country Club

Scarborough, New York

Sample of an invitation to a wedding anniversary

BRIDAL SHOWER INVITATIONS

The modern bridal shower is a throwback to the days when a bride brought her dowry to the marriage. Provided by her father, the dowry made her more attractive to potential husbands and gave the newly married couple material goods and finances to help them start their new lives together. Modern bridal showers, attended by family and friends, allow today's brides and grooms to have the basic necessities to furnish their new homes.

Bridal showers are traditionally hosted by one or more of the bride's friends. Bridesmaids who are not relatives of the bride are frequently hostesses. In the past it was considered inappropriate for a family member to host the event as it may have appeared they were soliciting gifts for the bride at the bride's request.

However, today it's not uncommon for the bride's sister, mother, or aunt to give the shower. What's important is that the shower feels like a celebration of the pending union and not merely a gift-giving-and-gathering frenzy. Use your best judgment in determining what would be appropriate for your situation and circumstance.

Many bridal showers have gift themes, such as linens, kitchen, or lingerie. For older brides who already have a well-stocked home, kitchen, or boudoir, themes might include garden or travel. The invitation should reflect the type of shower being hosted and clearly state the theme if one is being used. Often a motif is incorporated to enhance the invitation and to reinforce the theme.

Susan Neely
cordially invites you
to a Bridal Shower
in honor of
Kathy Carlson
on Thursday, May fifteenth
at seven o'clock
17 Park Street
Andover, Massachusetts

Susan Marie Neely
requests the pleasure of your company
at the Bridal Shower in honor of
KATHERINE ANNE CARLSON
Thursday, the fifteenth of May
at seven o'clock
17 Park Street
Andover, Massachusetts

We'd like to help Katherine and Rob with their new landscaping.
They are registered at Whiteflowerfarm.com.

Samples of bridal shower invitations

BABY SHOWER INVITATIONS

The guidelines for baby showers are similar to those for bridal showers.

Sample of a baby shower invitation

COMMENCEMENT INVITATIONS

Commencement invitations are sent on behalf of a school or university, inviting family and friends to the graduation ceremony.

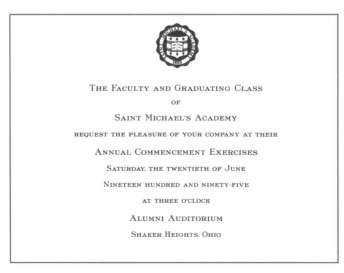

Sample of a commencement invitation

DEBUTANTE INVITATIONS

Young women are traditionally presented to society at a debutante ball. They may be presented at a private ball or along with other young women at a mass ball or cotillion. Due to the expenses involved, group balls are much more prevalent.

There are a series of events leading up to the debutante ball including dinners, teas, tea-dances, and small dances.

Dinner

A debutante dinner party honors the debutante and is given during the social season preceding the debutante ball.

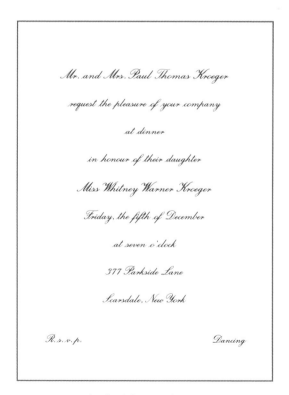

Mr. and Mrs. Paul Thomas Kroeger

request the pleasure of your company

at dinner

in honour of their daughter

Miss Whitney Warner Kroeger

Friday, the fifth of December

at seven o'clock

377 Parkside Lane

Scarsdale, New York

R.s.v.p.   Dancing

Sample of a debutante dinner invitation

Tea

Teas are given in the late afternoon. The phrase "At Home" is used to indicate that the invitation is for a tea. The tea is usually held for women of the debutante's mother's generation and older.

Mr. and Mrs. Paul Thomas Kroeger

Miss Whitney Warner Kroeger

At Home

Saturday, the sixth of November

at five o'clock

Sample of a debutante tea invitation

Tea Dance

The tea-dance is held for the debutante's friends.

Mr. and Mrs. Paul Thomas Kroeger

Miss Whitney Warner Kroeger

At Home

Saturday, the sixth of November

at five o'clock

Dancing

Sample of a debutante tea-dance invitation

Small Dance

A small dance is a dance of any size, large or small, given to honor the debutante.

> Mr. and Mrs. Paul Thomas Kroeger
> request the pleasure of your company
> at a small dance in honour of
> Miss Whitney Warner Kroeger
> Saturday, the second of December
> at nine o'clock
> Sleepy Hollow Country Club
> Scarborough, New York

Sample of a small dance invitation

Cotillion

A cotillion is a group ball during which a number of young women debut.

> The Governors of Sleepy Hollow
> request the pleasure of the company of
> Miss April Lee Fairbanks
> at a ball
> Saturday, the ninth of December
> at nine o'clock
> Sleepy Hollow Country Club
> Scarborough, New York

Sample of a cotillion invitation

BAR/BAT MITZVAH INVITATIONS

"Bar mitzvah" and "bat mitzvah" mean son of the commandments and daughter of the commandments respectively. A bar mitzvah is a boy who, upon reaching the age of thirteen, has attained the age of religious duty and responsibility. Bar mitzvah is also the name of the religious ceremony that is performed to recognize the attainment of religious maturity. A bat mitzvah (Hebrew) or a bas mitzvah (Yiddish) is a girl who achieves religious maturity, also at the age of thirteen. Bat mitzvah and bas mitzvah also refer to the ceremony.

While there is no standard etiquette for a bar or bat mitzvah invitation, some people believe it's important that the invitation reflect the sacred religious aspects of the ceremony and event. Others, however, prefer that the invitation reflect the spirit and interests of the young man or woman for whom the event is being held. It is not uncommon for invitations to be printed on vibrant colored papers with motifs.

Bar and bat mitzvah invitations are typically accompanied by a reply card and envelope (see page 89). If the celebration is being held at a location other than the temple, you will need to provide a direction or map card (see page 97).

Mr. and Mrs. Samuel Greenberg
request the honour of your presence
at the bar mitzvah of their son
Steven
Saturday, the seventh of April
at ten o'clock
Temple Beth Israel
Palm Beach, Florida

Luncheon following the services

Sample of a bar mitzvah invitation

QUINCE AÑOS INVITATIONS

A quince años is a traditional Hispanic celebration that marks a young woman's fifteenth birthday and her transition from childhood to adulthood. The celebration traditionally begins with a religious ceremony followed by a reception at home or at a banquet hall.

Invitations may be issued by the young woman being honored, the quinceanera, or her family. Formats vary dramatically based on the scale of the event and preference of the honoree.

Typical invitations include an outside envelope with an inside envelope that holds the invitation, reception card, reply card, and reply envelope. Some invitations may be printed in both English and Spanish to honor the tradition's roots and to accommodate Spanish-speaking guests.

The same rules that guide addressing wedding invitations (see page 43) apply to quince años invitations.

<table>
<tr><td>

SAMPLE #1:

Mr. and Mrs. Wesley Ortiz
have the honour to invite
you and your esteemed family
to the celebration of the
fifteenth birthday of their daughter
Lisa Marie
The Holy Mass in her honor
will take place on
Sunday, the fifth of May
Two thousand and seven
at one o'clock in the afternoon
Saint John's Church
Wrentham, Massachusetts

</td><td>

SAMPLE #2:

My joy will be complete
if you can share with me
the celebration of my
Fifteenth Birthday
in the presence of my parents
Mr. and Mrs. Ramon Gonzalez
A Holy Mass will be celebrated
in my honor
on Sunday, the eighth of January
two thousand and seven
at two in the afternoon
Saint John's Cathedral
One Main Street
Boston, Massachusetts

Julia Patricia

</td></tr>
</table>

SWEET SIXTEEN INVITATIONS

Sweet Sixteen celebrations can be quite formal or completely casual. The invitation should reflect the nature and theme of the event.

There are no rules regarding the format for sweet sixteen invitations. They can be professionally printed or produced at home with a quality printer using colorful papers and lined envelopes. Some people like to phrase their invitations in the form of a poem while others prefer a more traditional invitation style. Regardless of the language, information regarding the date, time, location, R.S.V.P. information, and so on must be included.

FILL-IN INVITATIONS

Fill-in invitations are personalized invitations that leave blank the areas for some of the information, such as the event, the date, and the time. They are usually ordered in large quantities and are used as the occasion arises. The "missing" information is filled in by hand.

Fill-in invitations may also be purchased over the counter without any personalization.

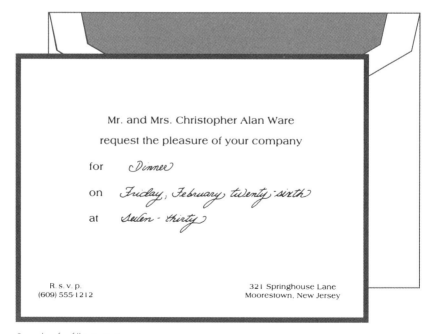

Sample of a fill-in invitation

SAVE-THE-DATE CARDS

Save-the-date cards are sent to guests who might need advance notification of an event so that they can make special arrangements. They are generally sent when an event is being held at a time when guests might otherwise make plans, such as holiday weekends. Save-the-date cards ask your guests to set aside that date for your event and are generally sent three to four months before the event. They do not take the place of invitations. The actual invitations are sent at a later date, usually four to six weeks before the event.

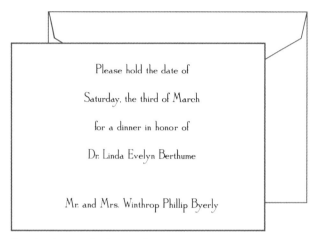

Sample of a save-the-date card

FORMAL REPLIES

Replies to the most formal invitations should be sent within three days of your receipt of the invitation or before the reply date given on the invitation. They are handwritten in black ink on your most formal stationery, such as a correspondence sheet, folded note, or correspondence card. The replies are written in the third person and follow the format of the invitation. They are sent to the persons issuing the invitation. If more than one name or a couple is listed, the replies are sent to whomever is listed first on the invitation.

Acceptances repeat the date and time. Regrets repeat just the date and may include a brief reason for not being able to accept. Mentioning the event is optional. If you do mention the event use "on" before the date. Otherwise, use "for."

Invitations from the White House always take precedence over other invitations. The only acceptable excuses for refusing invitations from the

White House are illness, a death in the family, a wedding in the family, and being out of the country.

ACCEPTANCE:

Mr. and Mrs. Taylor Randall Carr
accept with pleasure
the kind invitation of
Mr. and Mrs. Travis
to dinner
on Saturday, the sixth of June
at six o'clock

REGRET:

Mr. and Mrs. Taylor Randall Carr
regret that because of a previous commitment
they are unable to accept
the kind invitation of
etc.

ACCEPTANCE WITH CHILDREN:

Mr. and Mrs. Taylor Randall Carr
Esta, Janice, and Barbara
accept with pleasure
etc.

WIFE ACCEPTS, HUSBAND REGRETS:

Mrs. Taylor Randall Carr
accepts with pleasure
the kind invitation of
Mr. and Mrs. Travis
to dinner
for Saturday, the sixth of June
at six o'clock
Mr. Taylor Randall Carr
regrets that he is unable to accept
due to a previous commitment

INFORMAL REPLIES

Replies to informal invitations should be as formal or informal as the closeness of your relationship to the host or hostess dictates. For example, a reply sent to your mother should be a lot less formal than one sent to somebody you just met. If you are sending a regret, you should briefly state the reason. Replies should be made within three days and can be written on fold-over notes, correspondence cards, or even calling cards. If you use your calling cards, be sure to send them in an envelope that is large enough to mail. The smallest allowable mailing envelope measures $3\frac{1}{2}$" $\times$ 5".

The more traditional replies are written as in the following examples. If the invitation suggests another means of reply, such as by phone or email, you should do as your host asks.

ACCEPTANCE:
Mr. and Mrs. Taylor Randall Carr
accept with pleasure
the kind invitation of
Mr. and Mrs. Bolton
for Saturday, the sixth of June
at six o'clock

REGRET:
Mr. and Mrs. Taylor Randall Carr
regret that because of a previous engagement
they are unable to accept
the kind invitation of
Mr. and Mrs. Travis
for Saturday, the sixth of June

Mr. and Mrs. Jay Albert Greschree
accept with pleasure
the kind invitation of
Mr. and Mrs. Kimbrough
to dinner
on Friday, the third of December
at seven o'clock

Accept with pleasure
for Saturday, March 1st at 7:00

MR. AND MRS. JOHN TAYLOR COOPER

Regrets
for March 1st

MR. AND MRS. JOHN TAYLOR COOPER

Examples of replies prepared on
different styles of stationery

FILLING IN REPLY CARDS

Reply cards are sent with invitations in order to give recipients an easy and convenient way to respond. They should be returned promptly. Most cards feature a preprinted "M" before a line on which you are expected to write your name. You should complete your title using the "M" with "Miss," "Mrs.," or "Mr." If you are a doctor, you may cross out the "M" and write in your title.

If you will be attending the event, the space between "will" and "attend" is left blank. If you will not be attending, write "not" in that space.

Please reply

M _____

will _____ attend

Sample of
a reply card

BEYOND THE INVITATION

Whether you are entertaining at home, at your club, or in a restaurant, you can enhance the elegance of your event by using menu cards, place cards, and table cards.

Menu Cards

The most elegant and formal menu cards are white or ecru cards bordered or edged in gold or silver. The menu may be handwritten or printed on the card. Your monogram, your organization's seal, or your company's logo may be engraved at the card's top. You may also use a decorative motif to add to the theme of the festivities such as a scallop shell for a seafood dinner or a cornucopia for a Thanksgiving feast. The dinner's menu is listed down the center of the card. The wines are listed on the left, aligned with their corresponding courses. Courses are listed in the order that they are served. It is not necessary to list condiment items like coffee, tea, bread, butter rosettes, and so on, on a menu card.

One card is usually placed at each guest's place setting. If there is a dinner program, the menu card may be included inside the program. Since many guests will take home the menu card as a memento, they are usually printed on a fine card stock.

For more casual events, a menu card printed on quality paper with your ink-jet printer can produce excellent results.

Sample of a menu card

Place Cards

Traditionally, place cards are small white or ecru cards that are generally trimmed in gold or silver. But today, with the expanded use of colored paper and inks, the design options are practically unlimited.

They are placed on the table to identify everyone's seat. They can be used at any events of any size, large or small, when they will simplify the seating process.

Small folded place cards, also known as tent cards, stand on their own with the guest's name facing the guest. Flat cards may be placed in holders or simply set against the water glass. Either style may be placed on the table above the plate.

· POINTS OF STYLE ·
Extra Cards, Extra Cautious

Be sure to have a number of blank place and table cards available at your event so that you can address any misspellings or last-minute changes.

Like menu cards, place cards may be embellished with your monogram, duogram, seal, logo, or appropriate motif. Your place cards should match your menu cards in decoration, printing method, lettering style, and ink color.

On a very formal place card, only the guest's honorific and surname appear: "Judge Clayton" or "Mrs. Pritchett." At an informal event, the honorific may be omitted and just given and surname will be written: "Troy Clayton" or "Christine Pritchett." At very casual events where everyone is on a first-name basis, just the given name will be written.

Less formally, but very typical at business meetings, events, and conferences are the larger tent cards (or table tents) that are prepared with the name on both sides, acting as a name card for other guests at the table to see. Such double-sided cards are useful to facilitate networking and business development.

Sample of a place card

Table Cards

Table cards are helpful at small receptions and essential for large ones. Also known as "take-in cards" or YASA cards (You Are Seated At), they are alphabetized by the guest's surnames and placed on a table outside the reception hall to direct your guests to their respective tables.

Your guest's name is written on the front of the envelope. His or her surname, preceded by an honorific (Mr., Ms., Doctor, Captain, etc.) is used. If you have more than one guest with the same surname, their given names are added. The table number is written on the card inside.

At business events, they are sometimes used without an envelope. Event planners like to put the table number in pencil in case table-seating arrangements need to be adjusted at the last minute.

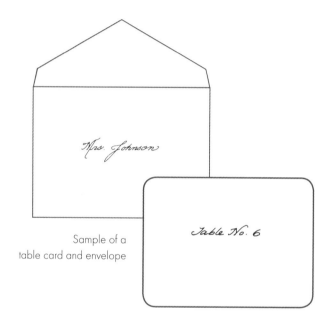

Sample of a
table card and envelope

CHAPTER SIX

Reception and Entertainment Stationery

An important part of being a good host or hostess is to anticipate your guests' needs and desires and to manage their expectations. Guests may wonder, "Where can I stay?" "How will I get from one event to another?" "Will I get a good seat?" "What's going to be served?" When you provide information that will be of interest to everyone in advance, both you and your guests' comfort levels will dramatically be increased.

And so, other stationery items are frequently created to complement the invitation and to add to the effortless appearance of the event. Here are some of the most frequently used items.

SAVE-THE-DATE CARDS

Save-the-date cards are sent to guests who might need advance notification of an event so that they can make special arrangements. They are generally sent when an event is being held at a time when guests might otherwise make plans, such as during the holiday or vacation seasons. Save-the-date cards ask your guests to set aside that date for your event and are generally sent three to four months before the event. They do not take the place of invitations. The actual invitations are sent at a later date, usually four to six weeks before the event.

Please hold the date of
Friday, the twentieth of August
for a dinner in honor of
Ms. Leah Hawthorn

Mr. Bruce Radford

TO REMIND CARDS

A "To Remind Card" is a confirmation sent to guests who have accepted an invitation extended by telephone, facsimile, or email. It is often sent to a guest of honor as a courtesy. Reminder cards are sent to arrive one week before the event.

Ms. Christina Travis
Director, Public Utilities Forum
cordially invites you to attend a dinner
in honor of
the Public Utilities Executives of the Year
on Wednesday, the eleventh of September
at half past six o'clock

To Remind   The Ritz-Carlton
                                             Tysons Corner

This is to remind you that
Ms. Christina Travis
is expecting you to dinner
Wednesday, the eleventh of September
at half past six o'clock
The Attaché Room
The Ritz-Carlton, Tysons Corner
1700 Tysons Boulevard
McLean, Virginia

REPLY CARDS

Many invitations include a reply card and envelope. Reply cards can be produced in a number of different formats. All formats, however, share similar features. Spaces are always provided for the guests' names and for their responses. A request for a response is always included as well, usually before a specific date. The reply request may be made in either the first two lines of the reply card or in the lower left-hand corner. The name and address of whoever will receive the replies appears on the face of the reply envelopes.

Omitting the "M" on a Reply Card

If an event is to be attended largely by individuals who do not use the honorifics Mr., Mrs., or Ms., such as members of the armed services, clergy, doctors, and certain elected officials, you may wish to omit the "M" on the reply cards. This leaves your reply cards with a blank name line and allows your guests to write in their appropriate titles.

REPLY ENVELOPES

Reply envelopes must always be included when a reply card is provided. The address of the issuer should appear on the face of the envelope. The inclusion of return postage is a matter of choice: many hosts and hostesses do include it as a courtesy to their guests, whereas government organizations are frequently prohibited from adding the postage.

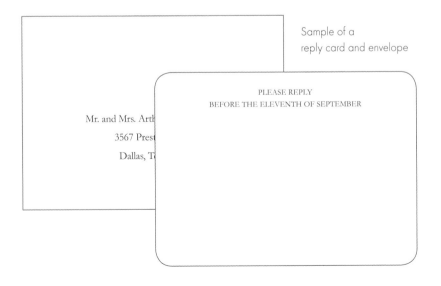

Sample of a
reply card and envelope

Mr. and Mrs. Arth

3567 Prest

Dallas, T

PLEASE REPLY
BEFORE THE ELEVENTH OF SEPTEMBER

DIRECTION AND MAP CARDS

If you are inviting individuals from out of town or who may not be familiar with the location of your event, a direction and/or map card will be appreciated. Direction cards give simple yet explicit driving instructions to your event, while map cards provide a map with the routes to your event location highlighted. Map cards generally feature major roads and landmarks to help your guests find their way. When direction cards or map cards accompany the invitation, the street address does not appear on the invitations.

As with other enclosures, direction cards and map cards should complement the invitations. They typically match the invitation style and color. To make them easier to read, a sans serif (block) lettering style is usually used.

Direction cards and map cards are usually sent with the invitation but may be sent afterward in an envelope or as a postcard to those who accept your invitation. When sent afterward, a line reading "We are looking forward to having you attend" may be added to the top of the cards.

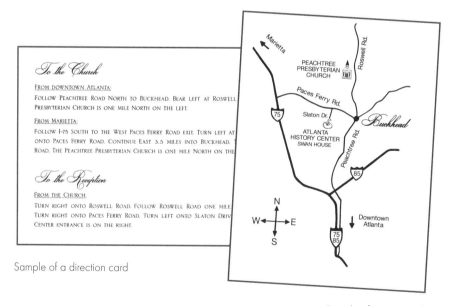

Sample of a direction card

Sample of a map card

ACCOMMODATIONS CARDS

Accommodations cards are enclosed with invitations sent to out-of-town guests who are unfamiliar with the area and need to make hotel reservations. They list the names and phone numbers of nearby hotels. If the hotel is offering a special room rate for the event, you may wish to include this information on the card.

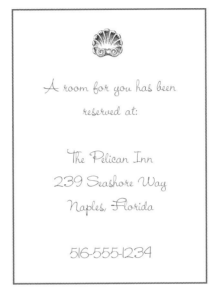

A room for you has been
reserved at:

The Pelican Inn
239 Seashore Way
Naples, Florida

516-555-1234

Sample of an
accommodations card

TRANSPORTATION CARDS

When a large number of out-of-town guests are attending an event, especially one in a big city, transportation from the hotel to the event is occasionally provided. Sent with the invitations, transportation cards let your guests know that their local travel plans have been taken care of. The cards generally read "Transportation will be provided / from the hotel to the event."

TRANSPORTATION WILL BE PROVIDED

FROM THE HOTEL TO THE EVENT

Sample of a
transportation card

SEATING TICKETS

Seating tickets are used when there are assigned seats. They are sent to the guest in advance and presented at the ceremony or event so the ushers can correctly and efficiently seat the guests. The pew or row and seat number can be written by hand in a space provided.

Please present this card at

Newport Beach Veterans Memorial Dedication Ceremony

Seaside Park Concourse

Monday, the fourth of July

Seat number: _____

Sample of a seating ticket

ADMISSION CARDS

Admission cards are a lot like tickets to the theater or to a ball game—you need to present them to gain admittance. Admission cards are generally used by well-known people who want to make sure that only invited guests are allowed to attend their event. They are sent with the invitations to all guests and may be personalized.

Please present this card at

Old Presbyterian Church

Saturday, the sixth of June

Mrs. Edward Cummings

will please present this card at

Newport Beach Veterans Memorial Dedication Ceremony

Seaside Park Concourse

Monday, the fourth of July

MENU CARDS

The most elegant and formal menu cards are white or ecru cards that are generally trimmed in gold or silver. The menu may be handwritten or printed on the card. Your monogram, your organization's seal, or your company's logo may be engraved at the card's top. You may also use a decorative motif to add to the theme of the festivities such as a scallop shell for a seafood dinner or a cornucopia for a Thanksgiving feast. The dinner's menu is listed down the center of the card. The wines are listed on the left, aligned with their corresponding courses. Courses are listed in the order that they are served. It is not necessary to list condiment items like coffee, tea, bread, butter rosettes, and so on, on a menu card.

One card is usually placed at each guest's place setting. If there is a dinner program, the menu card may be included inside the program. Since many guests will take home the menu card as a memento, they are usually printed on a fine card stock.

For more casual events, a menu card printed on quality paper with your ink-jet printer can produce excellent results.

PLACE CARDS

Traditionally, place cards are small white or ecru cards that are generally trimmed in gold or silver. But today, with the expanded use of colored paper and inks, the design options are practically unlimited.

They are placed on the table to identify everyone's seat. They can be used at any event when they will simplify the seating process.

Small folded place cards, also known as tent cards, stand on their own with the guest's name facing the guest. Flat cards may be placed in holders or simply set against the water glass. Either style may be placed on the table above the plate.

Like menu cards, place cards may be embellished with your monogram, seal, logo, or appropriate motif. Your place cards should match your menu cards in decoration, printing method, lettering style, and ink color.

On a very formal place card, only the guest's honorific and surname appear: "Judge Clayton" or "Mrs. Pritchett." At an informal event, the honorific may be omitted and just given and surname will be written: "Troy Clayton" or "Christine Pritchett." At very casual events where everyone is on a first-name basis, just the given name will be written.

Less formally, but very typical at business meetings, events, and conferences are the larger tent cards (or table tents) that are prepared with the name on both sides, acting as a name card for other guests at the table to see. Such double-sided cards are useful to facilitate networking and business development.

TABLE CARDS

Table cards are helpful at small receptions and essential for large ones. Also known as "take-in cards" or YASA cards (You Are Seated At), they are alphabetized by the guests' surnames and placed on a table outside the reception hall to direct your guests to their respective tables.

Your guest's name is written on the front of the envelope. His or her surname, preceded by an honorific (Mr., Ms., Doctor, Captain, etc.) is used. If you have more than one guest with the same surname, their given names are added. The table number is written on the card inside.

At business events, they are sometimes used without an envelope. Event planners like to put the table number in pencil in case table-seating arrangements need to be adjusted at the last minute.

ESCORT CARDS

An escort card is a card received by a guest at a dinner event on which is written the name of another guest and their joint table assignments. The card is typically presented inside a small envelope with the name of the guest on the outside front. The addressee is to find the other guest and escort that guest from the pre-dinner reception to dinner, where they will be seated together. The use of escort cards provides seating information and increases socialization by breaking up preexisting couples and introducing more guests to one another.

CHAPTER SEVEN

Social Announcements, Correspondence, and Cards

BIRTH ANNOUNCEMENTS

When a child is born, it is customary to send announcements heralding the event. Your choice of birth announcements should reflect your personality. They can be formal and traditional, or less formal and more imaginative.

The most traditional birth announcements are small cards that are attached to larger cards with a pink or blue ribbon. Other traditional announcements may be simple flat cards with a standard format with formal wording.

Less formal announcements can run the gamut from an adorable photo to an imprint of the baby's foot.

The titles "Mr. and Mrs." are used on the most formal announcements, but are dropped on less formal ones. A mother who uses her maiden name has her name appear on the line above the father's name. She does not use a title.

ADOPTION ANNOUNCEMENTS

Adoption announcements have the same look and format as birth announcements, but contain additional information. They typically include both the date of birth and the date on which the child was brought home.

WE ARE SO PLEASED TO ANNOUNCE
THE ARRIVAL OF OUR LITTLE BUNNY

MADELYN RORK CRAIG

JULY 11, 2012
7LBS. 11OZ.
19 INCHES OF PURE SWEETNESS

Samples of
birth announcements

Jordan Elizabeth Spencer

Seven pounds, fourteen ounces   May 3, 2002

Mr. and Mrs. James Ryan Spencer

Mr. and Mrs. Robert Thomas Farley

are happy to announce that

Patricia Ryan

joined their family

at five days of age

July 9, 2003

Samples of
adoption announcements

and Mrs. Donald Edward Chafee

ake pleasure in announcing that

Jennifer Sue Foley

has been adopted as their daughter

and will hereafter be known as

Jennifer Sue Chafee

February 16, 2013   April 27, 2013

Sometimes the word "arrived" is used instead of "adopted" as the adoption might not have been finalized before the arrival date. Many parents send adoption announcements as soon as they bring their child home while others wait until the adoption has been legally finalized. If the adoption involves a name change (as with an older child), the announcements generally mention the change.

CHRISTENING INVITATIONS

Christening and baptismal invitations are usually very informal. They may be printed in a standard format, engraved in the format of a personal note, or handwritten.

Mr. and Mrs. James Patrick Smith
invite you
to the christening of their daughter
Stephanie
Sunday, the nineteenth of September
at eleven o'clock
Church of Saint Joseph
Seattle, Washington
Reception to follow at home

Stephanie will be christened on Sunday, the nineteenth of September at eleven o'clock at the Church of Saint Joseph. Please join us for this special occasion and for a small luncheon at our home after the service.

Denise and Jim Smith

Samples of christening invitations

CHANGE-OF-NAME ANNOUNCEMENTS

People who legally change their names because of divorce or other reasons may let others know by sending an announcement.

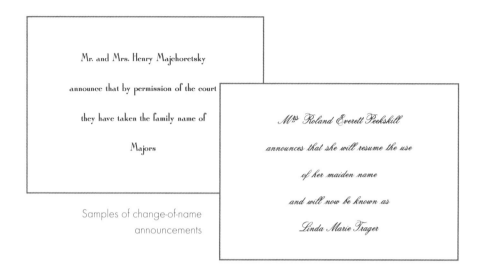

Mr. and Mrs. Henry Majchoretsky

announce that by permission of the court

they have taken the family name of

Majors

Samples of change-of-name
announcements

M�r⁵ Roland Everett Peekskill

announces that she will resume the use

of her maiden name

and will now be known as

Linda Marie Trager

CHANGE-OF-ADDRESS ANNOUNCEMENTS

Change-of-address announcements are sent to inform family and friends of your new address, phone number, and email address.

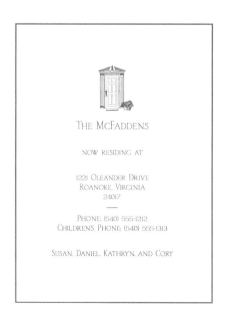

THE MCFADDENS

NOW RESIDING AT

1221 OLEANDER DRIVE
ROANOKE, VIRGINIA
24017
—
PHONE: (540) 555-1212
CHILDREN'S PHONE: (540) 555-1313

SUSAN, DANIEL, KATHRYN, AND CORY

I'm new on

UPTOWN GIRL

Mariko Takara
214 63rd Street · 3F
New York
—
Tel: (212) 555-1212
E-Mail: takara@aol.com

Samples of change-of-address
announcements

HOLIDAY GREETING CARDS

Individuals, families, and businesses send holiday greeting cards toward the end of the year. While most are sent in December to coincide with Christmas and Chanukah, some are sent in November, usually by businesses, to coincide with Thanksgiving.

Holiday cards come in many different styles and formats.

Businesses typically send cards with seasonal greetings as opposed to religious messages.

Families and individuals may choose religious or seasonal greetings. Photo cards are another popular option. Photo cards come in several different styles. Photo frames feature a preprinted or embossed frame in which an image is inserted. Photomount cards come with mounting tape that allows you to attach an image to the card.

Also available are digitally printed holiday cards, making use of your digital photography.

Your holiday cards may be personalized by adding your name or your company's name to the sentiment. Cards sent by a couple show the couple's first names followed by their surname. The woman's name appears first. Couples that do not share the same surname list their names on separate lines. Again, the woman's name appears first. Children's names may appear in age order (older to younger) on the same line together with their parents' names or separately on a second line.

MARRIED COUPLE:
Jeanette and Scott Robison
or
Mr. and Mrs. Scott Robison

COUPLE WITH DIFFERENT SURNAMES: Jeanette Baker
Scott Robison

CHILDREN'S NAMES:
Jeanette, Scott, Mindy, and Tina Robison
or
Jeanette and Scott Robison
Mindy and Tina

SAMPLE GREETINGS:

Merry Christmas
and a
Happy New Year

Season's Greetings
and
Best Wishes for the New Year

Wishing you joy and happiness
during this holiday season
and throughout the New Year

Wishing you a joyous Christmas
with health and happiness
through the coming year

May you find
health, happiness, and peace
during this Holiday Season
and through the coming year

ROSH HASHANAH CARDS

Cards celebrating the Jewish New Year are sent early enough to arrive before the holiday. Like other holiday cards, they may be sent by individuals, families, or on behalf of corporations.

Rosh Hashanah cards may be personalized by adding your name or your company's name to the sentiment. Cards sent by a couple show the couple's first names followed by their surname. The woman's name appears first. Couples that do not share the same surname list their names on separate lines. Again, the woman's name appears first. Children's names may appear in age order (older to younger) on the same line together with their parents' names or separately on a second line.

MARRIED COUPLE:	Judy and Bob Nishman
COUPLE WITH DIFFERENT SURNAMES:	Judy Goldstein Bob Nishman
CHILDREN'S NAMES:	Judy, Bob, Steven, and Bill Nishman or Judy and Bob Nishman Steven and Bill
SAMPLE GREETINGS:	All good wishes for health and happiness through the coming year May the coming New Year bring you health and happiness

THANK-YOU NOTES

A gift or act of kindness should be acknowledged as soon as possible. Your appreciation seems much more sincere when it is expressed promptly. Notes should be sent to thank someone for sending a gift, having you as a guest for dinner, or for any small favor. If you are not sure whether or not a thank-you note is called for, send one anyway. A note of appreciation is always welcome.

• POINTS OF STYLE •

Timing Is Everything

Write a thank-you note within twenty-four hours of an occasion while everything is fresh in your memory. A handwritten note will make you appear attentive, professional, and sincere in your thanks.

There's really no end to the number of choices you have in terms of style for your thank-you notes. Tradition dictates the use of a fold-over note with a monogram on the front and these are, of course, appropriate for all uses. However, you should feel free to select a note in a style that is a bit more reflective of your personality. Correspondence cards are also a popular option for thank-yous.

Sometimes it's best to have a few choices in your stationery wardrobe, using the most traditional notes for older relatives and others you are not that close to, and less traditional notes for extending thanks to close friends and family.

The message is usually brief and generally consists of five parts:

THE GREETING:

    Dear Barbara,

AN APPRECIATION OF THE GIFT OR FAVOR:

    Thank you for the beautiful, hand-carved walking stick.

MENTION HOW USEFUL IT WILL BE:

    It's already a reliable companion on my daily constitutional.

SUGGEST A FUTURE MEETING:

    I hope you'll find time to join me for a walk.

CLOSING: Love, Dad

INVITATIONS TO A MEMORIAL SERVICE

A memorial service is given in memory of the deceased. It may be given any time after the burial or cremation. The invitations are formal: black ink on an ecru or white card.

> 1923   2005
>
> In memoriam
> John Alexander Holmes
>
> The honor of your presence
> is requested at a memorial service
> Wednesday, the twenty-first of January
> at seven o'clock
> First Methodist Church
> Grove City, Pennsylvania

Sample of a memorial
service invitation

CONDOLENCE NOTES

Condolence notes are letters of sympathy sent to the family of the deceased. They should be sent on a timely basis and should contain sincere expressions of sympathy. Since condolence notes are sent at a difficult time for the family, they should be brief. They should contain personal praise of the deceased and, if appropriate, mention how life was enriched because of him or her. It is always appropriate to end with an offer to be of service to the family.

Dear Tom,

I was so sorry to hear about your father's death. I'll always remember playing ball with him in your backyard and his teaching us to always give our best. I'll miss him greatly.

If there is anything I can do, please let me know.

Sincerely,
Rick

Dear James,

Michael and I are deeply saddened by Melissa's death. Good friends are hard to come by and Melissa was the best. We will always miss her friendship and love.

Please call us if there is anything you need. We're always available.

Love,
Paula

Dear Mrs. Schwartzman,

We were all surprised and saddened by your husband's death. Working for him was a pleasure for all of us. His door was always open to us whenever we had a question or a problem. Coming to work will be a little bit harder for us now.

We hope you will still stop by and visit us when you're in the city.

Sincerely,
Susan Miller

SYMPATHY ACKNOWLEDGMENTS

Sympathy acknowledgments are handwritten notes of appreciation sent to family, friends, and business associates who expressed their condolences. They may be engraved when sent to people who are not known personally by the family or when an overwhelming number of acknowledgments need to be sent. A personal message may always be added to engraved acknowledgments.

Ecru or white cards are generally used for sympathy acknowledgments. They may be plain or bordered in black. At one time, the width of the border signified the sender's closeness to the deceased.

Mrs. Timothy Warren Chandler

wishes to express her appreciation

and sincere thanks

for your kind expression

of sympathy

Sample of a sympathy acknowledgment

CALLING CARDS

Steeped in the ultra-formal Victorian code of social etiquette, calling cards have made a fashionable resurgence in our fast-paced 21st-century lives. They are the perfect personal introduction for those occasions when a business card is too business-like.

Today calling cards are also used as a convenient means of sharing contact information, especially among singles, young mothers for play dates, retirees, and anyone needing to "network" out of the office. They can be produced in square, fold-over, and even die-cut formats. Cards often include an address, home phone number, cellular phone number, or email address. They may include as much, or as little, information as you feel comfortable with.

If your calling cards are to be used as a gift enclosure, you may want to order matching envelopes.

Calling Cards for Men

The information that follows is for the most traditional and formal calling cards for men. If these guidelines seem too formal, feel free to create cards in a style that best reflects your personality.

A man's full name, preceded by his title, is always used. His middle name is always spelled out, never abbreviated. While "Mr." is always abbreviated, other titles, such as "Doctor" and "Colonel," are spelled out. Suffixes, such as "junior," may follow the name. A man is a junior when he shares the same name as his father. He uses junior until his father passes away. Then, he drops it from his name. If, however, his father were a well-known figure, he would continue to use "junior" to avoid any confusion. It may appear in its abbreviated form as "Jr." or, when space permits, spelled out as "junior." When abbreviated, the "J" is capitalized. When spelled out, the "j" is lowercase.

A man uses "II" when he is named after an older relative other than his father; "III" is used when a man is named after somebody who uses "junior" or "II." They are usually preceded by a comma, although some men omit the comma. Traditionally, both formats are correct.

Mr. Griffen Alexander Greylock

Mr. Griffen Alexander Greylock, junior

Mr. Griffen Alexander Greylock, Jr.

Mr. Griffen Alexander Greylock, III

Calling Cards for Boys

A title does not precede the name of a boy under the age of eighteen.

Thomas Arthur Hancock

Calling Cards for Women

Married Woman

A married woman uses her husband's full name, preceded by "Mrs." Her husband's middle name is always included and is never replaced by his middle initial. If her husband's name is followed by a suffix, such as "Jr.," that suffix appears on her calling cards as well.

Mrs. Harrison Raiford Booth
Mrs. Harrison Raiford Booth, Jr.

Widows

A widow continues to use her husband's name on her calling cards. If her son is a junior who has dropped the "Jr." from his name, she adds the suffix, "senior" to distinguish herself from her daughter-in-law. "Senior" may be spelled out with a lower case "s" or abbreviated with a capital "S."

Mrs. Harrison Raiford Booth
Mrs. Harrison Raiford Booth, senior
Mrs. Harrison Raiford Booth, Sr.

Divorced Woman

A divorced woman uses her first name, maiden name, and married name, preceded by "Mrs." She may also use her first, maiden, and married names without a title.

Mrs. Lydia Renner Booth
Lydia Renner Booth

A divorced woman who resumed the use of her maiden name uses her first name, middle name, and last name, without a title.

Lydia Anne Renner

• POINTS OF STYLE •
The Use of "Ms."

In most circles, "Ms." does not properly appear on calling cards. If a woman feels uncomfortable using "Miss" or "Mrs.," she may omit her title.

Single Woman

A single woman typically uses her first name, middle name, and last name, preceded by "Miss." She may also omit her title.

Miss Lydia Anne Renner

Lydia Anne Renner

Calling Cards for Couples

Whether united through marriage or a civil union, many couples opt for a calling card that represents them as a couple. These cards may feature a duogram highlighting both sets of initials, their names in full, or simply their first names and other contact information. No matter the style, the important thing is that both parties feel comfortable using the card as a part of their personal introduction.

The most traditional couples calling card used by a married man and woman has "Mr. and Mrs." followed by the husband's first name, middle name, and last name. His middle name is always spelled out, never abbreviated. If the husband has a title other than "Mr." that title is used instead. Titles other than "Mr." and "Mrs." should not be abbreviated. When a name is too long to fit on a calling card, it is preferable to omit the middle name rather than to abbreviate a title or use an initial.

Mr. and Mrs. Harrison Raiford Booth

The Reverend and Mrs. Harrison Booth

Calling Cards for Medical Doctors

Physicians, surgeons, and dentists use the prefix "Doctor" or "Dr." on their calling cards. Professional degrees, however, should not appear on social cards.

A single woman who is a medical doctor or a married woman who has retained the use of her maiden name or who uses a professional name uses her first name, middle name, and last name, preceded by "Doctor" or "Dr."

A married woman who is a doctor traditionally uses her husband's given name, middle name, and surname, preceded by "Mrs." in social settings. Today, she is more likely to choose her given name, maiden name, and married surname, or to continue to use her full maiden name preceded by "Doctor" or "Dr."

MAN:	Doctor Jeffrey Allen Glenwood
	Dr. Jeffrey Allen Glenwood
SINGLE WOMAN:	Doctor Leslie Jean Carpenter
	Dr. Leslie Jean Carpenter
MARRIED WOMAN:	Mrs. Jeffrey Allen Glenwood
	Doctor Leslie Carpenter Glenwood
	Dr. Leslie Carpenter Glenwood

Calling Cards Using University and College Titles

Calling cards for general social use for college and university faculty members show no academic titles or degrees. However, calling cards intended for college and university use do show academic titles. The titles are never abbreviated. If there is not enough room on the card due to a long name and title, the middle name may be abbreviated. Letters indicating advanced degrees do not appear.

| GENERAL SOCIAL USE: | Mr. Gregory Winston Hughes |
| COLLEGE AND UNIVERSITY USE: | Doctor Gregory Winston Hughes |

Calling Cards for Clergy

Members of the clergy use their full names preceded by a courtesy title such as "The Reverend," or "The Most Reverend" as appropriate for their office or "Rabbi" if they are Jewish. Abbreviations are never used. Neither hierarchical ranks such as "Bishop" or "Monsignor," nor post-nominal abbreviations for advanced degrees or religious orders appear.

Rabbi Nathan Weisman
The Reverend John Kenneth Rhoads

CHAPTER EIGHT

Forms of Address

Federal Officials

GENERAL GUIDELINES

HANDLING THE NAMES OF SPOUSES OR PARTNERS OF OFFICIALS
For husbands use: Mr. (first name) + (last name)
Senator Helen Kinney and Mr. Robert Kinney
For women using their husband's last name use: Mrs. (last name)
Senator Robert Kinney and Mrs. Kinney
For women using a different last name use: Ms./Doctor/Miss (first name) + (last name)
Senator Robert Kinney and Ms. Helen Walters
For anyone using a different last name use: Mr./Ms./Doctor/Miss/etc. (first name) + (last name)
Senator Robert Kinney and Mr. Mark Henderson
Senator Helen Smith and Ms. Cynthia Parker

THE PRESIDENT OF THE UNITED STATES

	MAN	WOMAN
INVITATION	The President and Mrs. Smith	The President and Mr. Smith
OUTSIDE ENVELOPE	The President and Mrs. Smith	The President and Mr. James Smith
INSIDE ENVELOPE	The President and Mrs. Smith	The President and Mr. Smith

FORMER PRESIDENT OF THE UNITED STATES

	MAN	WOMAN
INVITATION	Mr. and Mrs. Smith	Mr. and Mrs. Smith
OUTSIDE ENVELOPE	The Honorable James Smith and Mrs. Smith	The Honorable Jane Smith and Mr. James Smith
INSIDE ENVELOPE	Mr. and Mrs. Smith	Mr. and Mrs. Smith

THE VICE PRESIDENT OF THE UNITED STATES

	MAN	WOMAN
INVITATION	The Vice President and Mrs. Smith	The Vice President and Mr. Smith
OUTSIDE ENVELOPE	The Vice President and Mrs. Smith	The Vice President and Mr. James Smith
INSIDE ENVELOPE	The Vice President and Mrs. Smith	The Vice President and Mr. Smith

MEMBER OF THE CABINET

	MAN	WOMAN
INVITATION	The Secretary of State and Mrs. Smith	The Secretary of State and Mr. Smith
OUTSIDE ENVELOPE	The Secretary of State and Mrs. Smith	The Secretary of State and Mr. James Smith
INSIDE ENVELOPE	The Secretary of State and Mrs. Smith	The Secretary of State and Mr. Smith

UNITED STATES SENATOR

	MAN	WOMAN
INVITATION	Senator Smith and Mrs. Smith	Senator Smith and Mr. Smith
OUTSIDE ENVELOPE	The Honorable James Smith and Mrs. Smith	The Honorable Jane Smith and Mr. James Smith
INSIDE ENVELOPE	Senator Smith and Mrs. Smith	Senator Smith and Mr. Smith

THE SPEAKER OF THE HOUSE

	MAN	WOMAN
INVITATION	The Speaker of the House and Mrs. Smith	The Speaker of the House and Mr. James Smith
OUTSIDE ENVELOPE	The Speaker of the House and Mrs. Smith	The Speaker of the House and Mr. James Smith
INSIDE ENVELOPE	The Speaker of the House and Mrs. Smith	The Speaker of the House and Mr. Smith

MEMBER OF THE HOUSE OF REPRESENTATIVES

	MAN	WOMAN
INVITATION	Mr. and Mrs. Smith	Mr. and Mrs. Smith
OUTSIDE ENVELOPE	The Honorable James Smith and Mrs. Smith	The Honorable Jane Smith and Mr. James Smith
INSIDE ENVELOPE	Mr. and Mrs. Smith	Mr. and Mrs. Smith

THE CHIEF JUSTICE OF THE SUPREME COURT

	MAN	WOMAN
INVITATION	The Chief Justice and Mrs. Smith	The Chief Justice and Mr. Smith
OUTSIDE ENVELOPE	The Chief Justice and Mrs. Smith	The Chief Justice and Mr. James Smith
INSIDE ENVELOPE	The Chief Justice and Mrs. Smith	The Chief Justice and Mr. Smith

ASSOCIATE JUSTICE OF THE SUPREME COURT

	MAN	WOMAN
INVITATION	Justice Smith and Mrs. Smith	Justice Smith and Mr. Smith
OUTSIDE ENVELOPE	Justice Smith and Mrs. Smith	Justice Smith and Mr. James Smith
INSIDE ENVELOPE	Justice and Mrs. Smith	Justice Smith and Mr. Smith

Diplomats

AMERICAN AMBASSADOR (AT POST, OUTSIDE THE WESTERN HEMISPHERE)

	MAN	WOMAN
INVITATION	The American Ambassador and Mrs. Smith	The American Ambassador and Mr. Smith
OUTSIDE ENVELOPE	The Honorable James Smith American Ambassador and Mrs. Smith	The Honorable Jane Smith American Ambassador and Mr. James Smith
INSIDE ENVELOPE	The American Ambassador and Mrs. Smith	The American Ambassador and Mr. Smith

AMERICAN AMBASSADOR (AT POST, IN THE WESTERN HEMISPHERE)

	MAN	WOMAN
INVITATION	The Ambassador of the United States of America and Mrs. Smith The Ambassador of the United States of America and Mr. Smith	
OUTSIDE ENVELOPE	The Honorable James Smith Ambassador of the United States and Mrs. Smith	The Honorable Jane Smith Ambassador of the United States and Mr. James Smith
INSIDE ENVELOPE	The American Ambassador and Mrs. Smith	The American Ambassador and Mr. Smith

AMERICAN AMBASSADOR (AWAY FROM POST, OUTSIDE THE WESTERN HEMISPHERE)

	MAN	WOMAN
INVITATION	Ambassador Smith and Mrs. Smith	Ambassador Smith and Mr. James Smith
OUTSIDE ENVELOPE	The Honorable James Smith American Ambassador to (country) and Mrs. Smith	The Honorable Jane Smith American Ambassador to (country) and Mr. James Smith
INSIDE ENVELOPE	Ambassador Smith and Mrs. Smith	Ambassador Smith and Mr. Smith

AMERICAN AMBASSADOR (AWAY FROM POST, IN THE WESTERN HEMISPHERE)

	MAN	WOMAN
INVITATION	Ambassador Smith and Mrs. Smith	Ambassador Smith and Mr. James Smith
OUTSIDE ENVELOPE	The Honorable James Smith Ambassador of the United States to (country) and Mrs. Smith	The Honorable Jane Smith Ambassador of the United States to (country) and Mr. James Smith
INSIDE ENVELOPE	Ambassador Smith and Mrs. Smith	Ambassador Smith and Mr. Smith

State & Municipal Officials

GOVERNOR

	MAN	WOMAN
INVITATION	The Governor of Iowa and Mrs. Smith	The Governor of Iowa and Mr. Smith
OUTSIDE ENVELOPE	The Governor of Iowa and Mrs. Smith	The Governor of Iowa and Mr. James Smith
INSIDE ENVELOPE	The Governor of Iowa and Mrs. Smith	The Governor of Iowa and Mr. Smith

STATE SENATOR OR REPRESENTATIVE

	MAN	WOMAN
INVITATION	Mr. and Mrs. Smith	Mr. and Mrs. Smith
OUTSIDE ENVELOPE	The Honorable James Smith and Mrs. Smith	The Honorable Jane Smith and Mr. James Smith
INSIDE ENVELOPE	Mr. and Mrs. Smith	Mr. and Mrs. Smith

MAYOR

	MAN	WOMAN
INVITATION	The Mayor of Dalton and Mrs. Smith	The Mayor of Dalton and Mr. Smith
OUTSIDE ENVELOPE	The Honorable James Smith and Mrs. Smith	The Honorable Jane Smith and Mr. James Smith
INSIDE ENVELOPE	The Mayor of Dalton and Mrs. Smith	The Mayor of Dalton and Mr. Smith

JUDGE

	MAN	WOMAN
INVITATION	Judge Knapp and Mrs. Knapp	Judge Sarah Knapp and Mr. Knapp
OUTSIDE ENVELOPE	The Honorable Harold Knapp and Mrs. Knapp	The Honorable Sarah Knapp and Mr. Harold Knapp
INSIDE ENVELOPE	Judge Knapp and Mrs. Knapp	Judge Knapp and Mr. Knapp

Religious Leaders

ROMAN CATHOLIC

	INVITATION	OUTSIDE ENVELOPE	INSIDE ENVELOPE
THE POPE	His Holiness, The Pope	His Holiness, The Pope	Your Holiness
CARDINAL	Cardinal Smith	His Eminence, John Cardinal Smith	Cardinal Smith
ARCHBISHOP	Archbishop Smith	The Most Reverend James Smith	Archbishop Smith
BISHOP	Bishop Smith	The Most Reverend James Smith	Bishop Smith
ABBOT	Abbot Smith	The Right Reverend James Smith	Abbot Smith
MONSIGNOR	Monsignor Smith	The Reverend Monsignor James Smith	Monsignor Smith
PRIEST	Father Smith	The Reverend James Smith	Father Smith

	INVITATION	OUTSIDE ENVELOPE	INSIDE ENVELOPE
BROTHER	Brother Smith	Brother James Smith	Brother James
MOTHER SUPERIOR USING FIRST AND FAMILY NAME	Mother Lesley	Mother Lesley Smith	Mother Lesley
MOTHER SUPERIOR USING CHOSEN RELIGIOUS NAME	Mother Mary Martha	Mother Mary Martha	Mother Mary Martha
SISTER USING FIRST AND FAMILY NAME	Sister Lesley	Sister Lesley Smith	Sister Lesley
SISTER USING CHOSEN RELIGIOUS NAME	Sister Mary Martha	Sister Mary Martha	Sister Mary Martha

EPISCOPAL

	INVITATION	OUTSIDE ENVELOPE	INSIDE ENVELOPE
PRESIDING BISHOP	Bishop Smith and Mrs. Smith	The Most Reverend James Smith and Mrs. Smith	Bishop Smith and Mrs. Smith
BISHOP (MAN)	Bishop Smith and Mrs. Smith	The Right Reverend James Smith and Mrs. Smith	Bishop Smith and Mrs. Smith
BISHOP (WOMAN)	Bishop Smith and Mr. Smith	The Right Reverend Jane Smith and Mr. James Smith	Bishop Smith and Mr. Smith
ARCH-DEACON (MAN)	Archdeacon Smith and Mrs. Smith	The Venerable James Smith and Mrs. Smith	Archdeacon Smith and Mrs. Smith
ARCH-DEACON (WOMAN)	Archdeacon Smith and Mr. Smith	The Venerable Jane Smith and Mr. James Smith	Archdeacon Smith and Mr. Smith
DEAN (MAN)	Dean Smith and Mrs. Smith	The Very Reverend James Smith and Mrs. Smith	Dean Smith and Mrs. Smith
DEAN (WOMAN)	Dean Smith and Mr. Smith	The Very Reverend Jane Smith and Mr. James Smith	Dean Smith and Mr. Smith

	INVITATION	OUTSIDE ENVELOPE	INSIDE ENVELOPE
CANON (MAN)	Canon Smith and Mrs. Smith	The Reverend Canon James Smith and Mrs. Smith	Canon Smith and Mrs. Smith
CANON (WOMAN)	Canon Smith and Mr. Smith	The Reverend Canon Jane Smith and Mr. James Smith	Canon Smith and Mr. Smith

PROTESTANT CHURCHES

NOTE: While Reverend is commonly used as an honorific in the manner of *Mr./Ms./Mrs./Dr.*, such use is not the correct traditional form. *Reverend* is a courtesy title and as such it describes an individual: This person is reverend.

Reverend is not traditionally used alone, with only a first or last name, or with a hierarchical title.

Correct traditional use would be *The Reverend Craig M. Phillips, pastor of St. Ann's Episcopal Church.* So by tradition, "Rev.," "Rev. Craig," "Rev. Phillips" would not be correct.

However, since personal preference is always taken into account, follow the preference of the bearer.

	INVITATION	OUTSIDE ENVELOPE	INSIDE ENVELOPE
MINISTER OR PASTOR (MAN) WITHOUT A DOCTORATE	Pastor and Mrs. Smith	The Reverend James Smith and Mrs. Smith	Pastor and Mrs. Smith
MINISTER OR PASTOR (WOMAN) WITHOUT A DOCTORATE	Pastor and Mr. Smith	The Reverend Jane Smith and Mr. James Smith	Pastor and Mr. Smith
MINISTER OR PASTOR (MAN) WITH A DOCTORATE	Dr. Smith and Mrs. Smith	The Reverend James Smith and Mrs. Smith	Dr. Smith and Mrs. Smith
MINISTER OR PASTOR (WOMAN) WITH A DOCTORATE	Dr. Smith and Mr. Smith	The Reverend Jane Smith and Mr. James Smith	Dr. Smith and Mr. Smith

CHURCH OF JESUS CHRIST OF LATTER-DAY SAINTS

	INVITATION	OUTSIDE ENVELOPE	INSIDE ENVELOPE
BISHOP OF A WARD	Mr. and Mrs. Smith	Mr. and Mrs. James Smith	Mr. and Mrs. Smith
BISHOP	Bishop and Sister Robinson	Bishop Stephen and Sister Robinson	Bishop and Sister Robinson
PRESIDENT OF A STAKE	President and Sister Robinson	President and Sister Stephen Robinson	President and Sister Robinson

SEVENTH-DAY ADVENTIST

	INVITATION	OUTSIDE ENVELOPE	INSIDE ENVELOPE
MINISTER	Elder and Mrs. Rojas	Elder Jose Rojas	Elder and Mrs. Rojas

JEWISH

	INVITATION	OUTSIDE ENVELOPE	INSIDE ENVELOPE
RABBI (MAN)	Rabbi and Mrs. Glass	Rabbi Neil Glass and Mrs. Glass	Rabbi and Mrs. Glass
RABBI (WOMAN)	Rabbi and Mr. Glass	Rabbi Miriam Glass and Mr. Neil Glass	Rabbi and Mr. Glass
RABBIS WHO ARE DOCTORS NOTE: Use of Rabbi usually supplants use of Dr., but sometimes in academia, or by personal preference, Rabbi Dr. is used.			
RABBI WITH DOCTORATE (MAN)	Rabbi Dr. and Mrs. Glass	Rabbi Dr. Neil Glass and Mrs. Glass	Rabbi Dr. and Mrs. Glass
RABBI WITH DOCTORATE (WOMAN)	Rabbi Dr. and Mr. Glass	Rabbi Dr. Miriam Glass and Mr. Neil Glass	Rabbi Dr. and Mr. Glass

	INVITATION	OUTSIDE ENVELOPE	INSIDE ENVELOPE
CANTOR (MAN)	Cantor and Mrs. Glass	Cantor Neil Glass and Mrs. Glass	Cantor and Mrs. Glass
CANTOR (WOMAN)	Cantor and Mr. Glass	Cantor Miriam Glass and Mr. Neil Glass	Cantor and Mr. Glass

HINDU

	INVITATION	OUTSIDE ENVELOPE	INSIDE ENVELOPE
PRIEST	Pandit Sri (name)ji	Pandit Sri (name)ji	Pandit Sri (name)ji

SHIITE

	INVITATION	OUTSIDE ENVELOPE	INSIDE ENVELOPE
IMAM	Sayyid (Sheikh) Al Borno	Sayyid (Sheikh) Mohamad Al Borno	Sayyid (Sheikh) Al Borno

SUNNI

	INVITATION	OUTSIDE ENVELOPE	INSIDE ENVELOPE
IMAM	Imam Shamsi Ali	Imam Mohamad Shamsi Ali	Imam Shamsi Ali

CHAPTER NINE

About Crane & Co., Inc.

In 1776, the Massachusetts Bay Colony issued the first colonial currency backed by a colony and not by the English Crown. Stephen Crane's Liberty Paper Mill produced the paper for those notes and sold them to the colonial government. Although better known for his midnight ride, Paul Revere engraved those first colonial notes.

In 1799, Stephen's son, Zenas Crane, headed west to search for a site for a mill of his own. He needed a place with an abundant supply of fresh water (for power and for cleansing the rags used in papermaking) and where the surrounding area would produce both an ample supply of rags for use as a raw material and a growing market. (Housewives saved their rags and sold them or bartered them to the general store. A rag merchant bought the rags and resold them to the paper mill, where they were transformed into paper.)

Zenas Crane's search ended in Dalton, Massachusetts, a small agricultural community nestled in the Berkshire hills. Dalton's location gave him the water he needed and access to southern markets through New York City and western markets through Albany, New York.

In partnership with John Willard and Henry Wiswall, Zenas Crane purchased a fourteen-acre site for the sum of $194. Crane & Co. was founded in 1801 when the new company placed an advertisement in the *Pittsfield Sun* asking ladies to save their rags.

Zenas Crane's company produced paper for businesses, printers, and publishers. He also sold paper to the independent banks that were authorized to print paper money.

Bond paper is a paper with a hard finish that is used for bonds, stock certificates, and business letterheads. The term was first used in 1850 when the president of a New York bank wrote to Crane asking for some "bond paper." The term soon became the generic term for the type of paper used for bonds.

Also at that time, paper money was being counterfeited by a process called raising, which was the illegal process of changing, for example, a one dollar bill into a ten dollar bill, by drawing a zero after the one on the bill. In 1844, Crane developed a technique to put silk threads in its banknote paper to prevent the raising of money. Crane put a single thread in one dollar bills, two threads in two dollar bills, and three threads in three dollar bills. If somebody held what appeared to be a ten dollar bill to the light and saw a single silk thread, he knew that the bill was counterfeit.

Crane's mastery of this innovative technique was instrumental in landing a contract in 1879 to supply the paper for the currency of the United States. Since that day, Crane has supplied virtually all U.S. currency paper to the United States Bureau of Engraving and Printing. Crane also supplies currency and banknote paper to international customers.

The company Zenas Crane founded in 1801 has grown, prospered, and diversified but is still owned by his descendants, still makes 100% cotton fiber stationery, and still adheres to the quality standards on which he insisted.

Crane products today include currency and security papers, nonwoven technical products, and a complete line of business and social stationery papers for corporate letterheads, social correspondence, invitations, and announcements. For more information, visit crane.com.

Index